SoulTypes

Matching Your Personality and Spiritual Path

D0380560

Sandra Krebs Hirsh
Jane A. G. Kise

MINNEAPOLIS

SOULTYPES
Matching Your Personality and Spiritual Path

Large-quantity purchases or custom editions of this book are available at a discount from the publisher. For more information, contact the sales department at Augsburg Fortress, Publishers, 1-800-328-4648, or write to: Sales Director, Augsburg Fortress, Box 1209, Minneapolis, MN 55440-1209.

Scripture quotations, unless otherwise marked, are from the *Holy Bible, New International Version,* copyright © 1973, 1978, 1984 International Bible Society. Used by permission of Zondervan Publishing House. All rights reserved.

Scripture quotations marked NLT are from the *Holy Bible, New Living Translation,* copyright © 1996. Used by permission of Tyndale House Publishers, Inc., Wheaton, Illinois 60189. All rights reserved.

Scripture quotations marked NRSV are from the *New Revised Standard Version of the Bible,* copyright © 1946, 1952, 1971, 1989 by the Division of Christian Education of the National Council of the Churches of Christ in the U.S.A. Used by permission.

Library of Congress Cataloging-in-Publication Data
Hirsh, Sandra Krebs.
  SoulTypes: matching your personality and spiritual path / Sandra Krebs Hirsh, Jane A. G. Kise.
    p. cm.
  Includes bibliographical references.
  ISBN 0-8066-5146-6 (pbk. : alk. paper)
  1. Spiritual life. 2. Typology (Psychology)—Religious aspects. 3. Myers-Briggs Type Indicator. I. Title: Soul types. II. Kise, Jane A. G. III. Title.
  BL627.57.H57 2005
  200.1'9—dc22   2005027098

Cover design by Diana Running; Cover photo © Photodisc/Getty Images. Used by permission; book design by Michelle L. N. Cook

The paper used in this publication meets the minimum requirements of American National Standard for Information Sciences—Permanence of Paper for Printed Library Materials, ANSI Z329.48-1984. ♾ ™

Manufactured in the U.S.A.

To all sojourners who, along with me,
are seeking enriched spirituality,
discovering who we are,
building on the gifts we've been given,
and appreciating the uniqueness of each person's journey.

—Sandra Krebs Hirsh

To my mom, Muriel Griffin,
whose love, encouragement, and deep faith
are a constant source of inspiration and motivation to me.

—Jane A. G. Kise

CONTENTS

FOREWORD

During her visits to see me, my daughter, an active, living-in-the-moment person, consistently turns aside invitations to join me in my various religious or spiritual activities. A white-water kayaker, she thanks me very much as she says, "My church is the woods and the rivers." With our family's deep heritage in the theory of psychological type and the gifts of our individual personalities, I can only respect my daughter's approach to spirituality!

Yet, along with Sandra Hirsh and Jane Kise, I have long been puzzled by the fact that several of the sixteen types virtually never appear at the workshops and programs I personally find most rewarding for my spiritual development. *SoulTypes* satisfies my long-standing curiosity as to how other people fulfill their desire for significance and purpose. I read it with growing excitement, a tour de force of effectiveness unscrolling as I turned each page.

The book is ambitious in what it attempts. Using the formulation of twentieth-century Swiss psychiatrist Carl Jung's psychological type, as developed by Katharine C. Briggs and Isabel B. Myers in the Myers-Briggs Type Indicator (MBTI)®, and through extensive conversations with individuals demonstrating each of the sixteen Jungian types, the authors have sketched portraits of the spiritual paths most natural to each type. The result is a book that can serve as an invaluable guide to an individual or a group working together on a journey of spiritual growth—a journey sparked by the universal yearning for meaning, balance, and connectedness to one another and to something greater than oneself.

As writers, Hirsh and Kise have managed to order what could be overwhelmingly complex materials and ideas, leading the reader in gentle, easy-to-understand steps into the richness of complexity, without sacrificing meaning for the sake of simplicity. By illuminating each step of spiritual development with the words of people telling their stories, the full richness of the dynamic and developmental aspects of psychological type is imparted.

As researchers, they worked to discover both the differences in spiritual concerns and the practices and patterns that might be common for each type. They shared with me that their role became one of "stewards for these messages" as they tried to let each type speak for itself, defining its unique approach to soulwork.

As authors, they live out, in every word, their respect for each individual and for each of the many valid paths toward growth and spiritual development. As a result, their book will speak to people of many faiths as well as to nonbelievers and skeptics who are questioning and open to exploration.

The book is carefully crafted for use in daily life and soulwork. The skill with which this is done reflects the authors' years of experience in workshop leadership and design. Readers will come to understand

- the many valid forms of spirituality;
- past frustrations with their spiritual history, opening doors to renewed exploration;
- the spiritual pathway most natural to them—one that brings the greatest joy, insight, clarity, and practical help; and
- ways to expand their spiritual practices, thus enriching the journey.

Readers will grasp their uniqueness as well as their commonality with others who possess a similar nature. Ideas gleaned from learning about other types will help to bring new creativity and interest to readers' individual pathways and their movement toward balance and wholeness.

In an early chapter, the authors confess to sharing a passion for helping others reach their full potential. I was reminded of Isabel B. Myers and her mother, Katharine C. Briggs, who found Jungian psychological type so useful in their own lives. Their mission in life became to enable others to have access to this knowledge through the MBTI®. Myers and Briggs gave others access to their preference type; Hirsh and Kise in *SoulTypes* have succeeded in providing a clear way of applying that understanding to the never-ending, lifelong process of spiritual growth and fulfilling living.

—Katharine D. Myers
Founding President, Association for Psychological Type

PREFACE

What can we do to help people discover the importance of spirituality? Of tapping into the intangible part of their lives? Of developing a relationship with God for meaning, fulfillment, growth, and shelter from the inevitable storms of life?

These questions arose from our discovery that there are definite patterns in the personalities of people who do and do not attend church, synagogue, or other spiritual communities. This book is our answer. We hope it is an answer that will resonate with anyone who is trying to help others find a vibrant spiritual path or who is seeking a deeper path.

Nearly fifteen years ago, Sandra decided to bring her vast experience with career development and coaching to her church, helping to design a seminar that became our book *LifeKeys: Discover Who You Are.*[1] That's where we met—and where our questions regarding how the rituals, traditions, practices, and forms of worship of many spiritual communities favor some personalities over others. Jane, a writer and strategic planning consultant, minored in religion in college and longed to put her talents and knowledge to use for the church. The first book we wrote together, *Work It Out* (Davies-Black, 1996, 2006) concerned teambuilding and executive coaching. However, the spiritual implications of using type intrigued us even more. We began interviewing people who had attended LifeKeys seminars, friends and family members, and people from around the world who were interested in both personality type and spirituality. Each person had identified his or her best-fit type. For each of the sixteen personality types, we tried to find at least seven people to interview, in different stages of life and with diverse religious backgrounds. We contacted our colleagues in the Association for Psychological Type, a worldwide organization with several thousand members, to help us find individuals who matched our criteria. Thus the stories include the views of people from all over the United States as well as from Australia, Canada, England, Korea, New Zealand, Singapore, and Sweden.

The style of interview differed from type to type—many of the people with a preference for Feeling had us over for coffee. Many Thinkers preferred to respond via e-mail. It made sense to us that their responses would be better if we honored their natural communication styles. We asked: What practices draw you closer to God? What pushes you away? What are your favorite ways to worship? Study? Pray? Serve? How has your spirituality changed over the years? What new practices are you discovering now?

We recorded their stories, both positive and negative experiences. We paid special attention to those who had turned their backs on the faiths of their childhood. What caused disillusionment? What enhanced their faith? As the patterns in answers emerged, we asked more people who were familiar with the theory of personality type to review the conclusions we were drawing. Did the spiritual path we were describing sound like them? Overwhelmingly, they said, "Yes—that explains my frustration." Or, "Yes. No wonder I find prayer so natural; my natural style is how I was taught to pray." Or, "No wonder my friend doesn't understand my faith—we're wired so differently that I need to explain things to her in a vastly different way."

Our findings became first the booklet *Looking at Type and Spirituality* (Center for Applications of Psychological Type, 1997), then the book *SoulTypes* (Hyperion, 1998). This is the second edition. Our goal was to make the text in this edition more accessible to people for whom the concepts of personality type are new. Also, we added more exercises, stories, and examples from the SoulTypes seminars we have taught since the first edition was published and a more complete study guide for using *Soul-Types* in small groups.

We could not have written this book without the assistance of friends, colleagues, and even strangers who were willing to share their personal stories, insights, and spiritual journeys to help us create accurate pictures of spirituality for each type. With their permission, we have quoted their stories throughout the book, though their names have been changed.

Our heartfelt thanks to Nancy Achterhoff, Sarah Albritton, Dana Alexander, Larry Atkinson, Lynn Baab, Lena Bakedahl, Maureen Bailey, Charette Barta, Randi Baxter, Monica Bergman, Paul and Nan Bertleson, Craig Blakeley, Robert Boozer, Polly Bowles, Christine Boyer, Nicky Bredeson, Amy Carrizo-Brennen, Susan Brock, Nancy Brooker, Helen Krebs Bruant, Joan Buchanan, Dee Cauble, Elizabeth Couble, Laura Crosby, Penny Davis, Jamelyn R. DeLong, Larry Demarest, Jean and Steve Diede, Jari Dostal, Debbie Ducar, Kit Duncan, Terry Duniho, Terri Elton, Binnie Ferrand, Margaret Fields, P. J. Fuller, Barb Gabbert, David D. Getsch, Peter Geyer, Linda Gilligan, Thomas Golatz, Richard D. Grant, Jr., Ken Green, Jean Greenwood, Eva Grollova, Ellen Griffin, Tom Griffin, Jack and Vicki Griffin, Jane Griffin, Muriel Griffin, Lonnie and Alison Gulden, Kay Hacklander, Madge Hanson, Becky Harris, Elizabeth Hirsh, Katherine Hirsh, Jeanne Hoagland, Diane Huling, Lee Hulsether, Greg Huszczo, Pat Hutson, Myra Hykes, Kevin Johnson, Mary Johnson, Karen Keefer, O. Fredrick Kiel, Christine King, Linda Kirby, Brian Kise, Brenda and Dean Knutson, Paula Kosin, Jindra Krpalkova, Jean Kummerow, Bob and June Kunzie, Alan Leggat, Rosemary Long, Sharon W. Lovoy, Sally and Rob Lund, John and Meredith Lundgren, Margarita Lycken, Peter Malone, Beverly Mease-Buxton, Jerry McDaid, Steve Merman, Wayne D. and Jan Mitchell, James Mullins, Steve and Jo Mundy, Andrew Murray, Laurie Nadel, Julie Neraas, Judith E. Nicholas, Ann and Bill Oliver, Tim Olsen, Barbara Olson, Kit Olson, Richard Olson, J. Sam Park, Sue Pepper, Peter Richardson, Helen Marie Plourde, William Rebholtz, Sally Riglar, Judy Ritchie, Ranelle Rulana, Josef Rzyman, JoAnne Sandler, Fred and Elsie Scaife, William F. Schmidt, Don Smith, Kurt Smith, Sandy Smith, David and Janet Stark, Grace Stewart, Karen Stuart, Randy A. Stricker, Shelley Thompson, Barbara Upton, Sondra Van Sant, Peggy Sue Vojtech, Jay Warren, Hichul Henry Whang, Bob Witherspoon, Carolyn and Ray Zeisset.

Sandra and Jane, along with the people whose stories enrich these pages, hope that this volume can bring new meaning and vitality to your spiritual journey, as they have to ours.

INTRODUCTION

PATHWAYS, PURSUITS, AND PRACTICES

A Pathway to Finding Your Natural Spiritual Path

Are you spiritual? Is this how you pray?

> *I felt communion, peace, openness to experience, . . . an awareness and responsiveness to God's presence around me, and a feeling of centering, quieting, nothingness, . . . moments of the fullness of the presence of God.*[1]

How about this?

> *Often when I look at an ordinary thing, something wonderful happens. I get the feeling that I am seeing it fresh for the first time. . . . Sometimes I have felt like I was part of something with no limits or boundaries in time and space.*[2]

A friend of ours, Steve, took a quiz in one of the above-quoted magazine articles and said, "I said 'false' to all of them. So I have no faith? Funny, given all the time I spend serving God!" Here's how he describes his prayer:

> *To me the issue was, if the universe is the answer, what was the question? My insights come from books and articles on quantum mechanics and the new physics—most helpful in cracking the code of our cosmos and providing insights into why we're here. But . . . I know*

people are shocked when I say that the most profound spiritual text I've read is Stephen Hawkings' A Brief History of Time!

Is he spiritual? Can quantum physics prompt prayer? What about this one?

I feel most spiritual during my exercise time—I know I'm doing something good for myself while at the same time I can also talk to God in prayer. Golf for example . . . I'm good at golf. I know which clubs to use, the lay of the ground, how to correct for the wind—shots go well and I feel alive.

Or how about this person?

I enjoy working on projects, often alone, that require ingenuity and improvisation—difficult issues that have the potential of getting to the root of problems. I often sense that God is trying to talk directly to me as I focus on the task—this is where I can do something of purpose with my life.

Can a person pray by serving?

For me, prayer is about action. Why pray if it doesn't lead to practical acts of love? When I am working for others, I am praying. When I am praying, I am working for others. At times I confess that I am so others-focused I forget that I need to pray for myself and to nurture my own soul as well, so I can continue to grow in love and wisdom.

In many, many circles, the answer to these questions is, "No." Spirituality is defined in just one way. Perhaps that way varies among churches, synagogues, and faiths, but still there is a sense of doing a spiritual journey, or what we call soulwork, the "right" way.

Is There a "Right" Way?

Look back at the first two quotations. A group of scientists interested in exploring whether there are brain-based differences that determine our affinity for religion are using the style of prayer described there to define who is and isn't "spiritual." In all religions, these neuroscientists say, mystical, spiritual moments happen when parts of the brain (parietal-lobe circuits) go quiet, turning off your ability to distinguish between the body and its surroundings. Without sensory data, you feel a sense of being part of infinity or, for the religious, being "one with God." They use SPECT scans (Single Photon Emission Computed Topography) of the brain to determine whether a person is having such an experience. Building on this research, books such as *The God Gene* describe how we either are or aren't wired for faith. Kenneth L. Woodward, a religion journalist for *Newsweek*, points out the problem with this approach:

> "The chief mistake these neurotheologians make is to identify religion with specific experiences and feelings. Losing one's self in prayer may feel good or uplifting, but these emotions have nothing to do with how well we communicate with God. In fact, many people pray best when feeling shame or sorrow, and the sense that God is absent is no less valid than the experience of divine presence."[3]

He's right. Under the neuroscience definition, convenient as it is for research purposes, would even King David qualify as spiritual? Would his prayers count as he poured out his heart?

> Have mercy on me, O God,
> because of your unfailing love.
> Because of your great compassion,
> blot out the stains of my sins. . . .
> Oh, give me back my joy again;
> you have broken me—
> now let me rejoice.
> —Psalm 51:1, 8; NLT

What about Hannah, who cried bitterly as she prayed, "If you will look upon my sorrow and answer my prayer and give me a son, then I will give him back to you" (1 Samuel 1:11). Does her begging, which resulted in the birth of the prophet Samuel, discount her from being spiritual?

Scientists aren't the only ones who narrow the definition of what is and isn't spiritual. As quoted earlier, quantum physics, golf, and acts of being of service are just a few of the ways people we have talked with have experienced profound connections with God. Here's the real problem with any narrow definition of who is and isn't spiritual: It alienates those who don't fit the definition from an essential part of their beings. Many of the people we interviewed who said, "I'm not very spiritual" had been *told* so by other people, either directly or by sensing that they didn't measure up to some standard of spirituality set by those around them or by the religion of their childhood.

Yet we all need a spiritual dimension. Our minds and our bodies aren't enough to successfully navigate through life; we need to access our souls as well. Carl Jung, the Swiss psychiatrist put it this way:

> People from all the civilized countries of the earth have consulted me. I have treated many hundreds of patients. Among all my patients in the second half of life—that is to say, over thirty-five—there has not been one whose problem in the last resort was not that of finding a religious outlook on life. It is safe to say that every one of them fell ill because he had lost that which the living religions of every age have given to their followers, and none of them has been really healed who did not regain his religious outlook.[4]

In other words, whether people know it or not, they need to tap into their souls. Further, life brings discoveries and events that simply cannot be explained by what we think, do, feel, or even imagine. In our view, spirituality taps the pursuits and ideas that allow for meaning, purpose, and wholeness in life. While these certainly include the mystical experiences that neuroscientists are studying and the rituals and practices present in many faiths, there is much, much more. Yet some people, whether through brainwave research, uncomfortable or even harmful religious experiences, or through being told, "Your thoughts are sinful!" have walked away from any sort of spiritual path. Further, because of the narrow definition of who's spiritually "in" and who's "out," patterns of spiritual alienation have emerged.

Personality type is a tool for understanding the different ways people take in information and make decisions about it.

The concepts are fully explained in chapter 1. But ponder what happens when we don't get the information we need or decisions are made in ways with which we disagree. Our personality type, therefore, has a profound effect on our spiritual experiences.

The Consequences of One Path

The two of us noted patterns in this spiritual alienation fifteen years ago when we began teaching our LifeKeys[5] classes, designed to help people find meaning and purpose in life. We devoted one session to personality type (see sidebar, page 16). Every time we offered the series, the same six personality types were consistently underrepresented or missing altogether among participants. We knew our materials met the needs of the missing types because we had used similar exercises in business for years. So why didn't they attend our LifeKeys sessions?

When we asked our professional colleagues in the personality-type community, they affirmed what we had noted: These same types are consistently absent from organized Western religious communities.

Given that our spiritual side, essential to navigating life's journey, doesn't scream for our attention the way that our bodies, our families, our work, or our pocketbooks do, the absence of these personality types struck us as fundamentally unjust. We know when we are hungry for food or water, but the needs of our souls can go undetected, especially if our early experiences with spirituality failed to feed us. We didn't think our loving Creator decided, "Hah! I'm going to make it really tough for throngs of people to know me, or to even believe I exist." No, we suspected that the practices espoused by different faiths had turned these people off.

So, we asked literally hundreds of people from all over the world who knew their personality types,

- What draws you toward God, faith, or spirituality?
- What pushes you away?

We talked with people from Protestant, Catholic, Jewish, Bahá'í, and Unitarian traditions, both those who chose to remain with their childhood faiths and those who decided those paths did not suit them. Among those who changed paths, we encountered both agnostics and atheists, listening carefully to their stories of where their spiritual paths had taken them.

The reaction among several people in the first group we talked with was, "What do you mean by spirituality?" So we researched various definitions and refined a meaning that resonated with our purpose of exploring spirituality in its infinite variety of manifestations. Here, *spirituality* refers to aligning our souls with heart, mind, and body to fulfill one's purpose, believing that reality includes more than the tangible, and it refers to pursuing a relationship with One greater than ourselves.

To make clear that we would be discussing practices and customs, rituals and forms of prayer—the ways in which we form our beliefs, not the beliefs themselves—we decided to use "soulwork" as a neutral phrase to define our spiritual paths. *Soulwork* means the pursuits and practices that allow for meaning, purpose, and wholeness in life, reaching beyond direct experiences to the unseen around us.

And, finally, while both of us actively pursue our spirituality within Christian communities, we broadened our definitions so that we could listen to those who had become alienated from the faith we hold dear. We talked about "religion" separately from soulwork. *Religion* refers to a way of pursuing soulwork by banding with others who espouse the same beliefs or creeds.

Once we clarified our definitions, our participants truly opened their hearts and souls to us, telling of past hurts, puzzlements, and theological land mines that had defined their spiritual paths—or lack thereof.

Their stories and examples bore out our premise that the sixteen personality types, which are explained in chapter 1, each had their unique slant on what it means to be spiritual. When that slant was honored in their early experiences, soulwork became important to them. When it was not, they left the church or other spiritual community, switched faiths, or did without—often until some crisis sent them searching for answers or comfort or community.

Our Purpose

Our research started with the simple question, "Why aren't some types present at our seminars?" and ended with, "How can we help *everyone* find the spiritual path that fits their personality?"

If you struggle with religion or faith, we hope that these pages might help you understand your past reactions to forms of worship, teaching, doctrine, or other spiritual practices.

If you have found your spiritual path, we hope that these pages will provide insights for going deeper as you move into the next stages of life.

If you hope to encourage others along their spiritual journeys, we hope that these pages will increase your awareness of the many valid forms of soulwork, some of which are distinctly different from what many organized religions—or the neuroscientists we quoted above—define as spiritual.

These pages lay out the spiritual paths of each of the sixteen MBTI® personality types, as much as possible in the words of the people themselves. Each of the pathways is a rich, lifelong journey of discovery full of new avenues for growth, not a single set of prescriptive practices. Further, we hope that the theory of personality type, the wisdom of those who shared their journeys with us, and the witness of their experiences will allow you to

- find those practices that bring the greatest joy, insight, clarity, help—whatever you need most from soulwork;
- understand your past frustrations with religion and spirituality;
- grant new freedom for yourself and others to take a different path;
- find comfort and strength in life's struggles;
- continue on a rich, fulfilling spiritual journey all of your days.

PART ONE

UNDERSTANDING PERSONALITY TYPE

CHAPTER ONE

FINDING YOUR NATURAL SPIRITUAL PATH

What kinds of information about spirituality are valuable or meaningful to you?

- Information that is easily verified?

  I know there's more to life than what I can see and touch, but to find my spiritual side, I have to look for evidence in the lives of others. For example, I watched the reaction of friends who lost their little boy to leukemia. Earthly reality would have made them collapse under the grief. Instead, the unseen dimension and support of their faith allowed them to function, to comfort their friends, and to love and nurture their other children. Their faith was real. Seeing their example, soul-work became urgent; I want to have that kind of spiritual base.
  —Dave, 32, teacher

- Information that goes beyond what is known?

  Because I'm curious, open, and a "possibility person," I love the whole idea of exploring those aspects of my life that I can't see or touch. The idea of God and the mysteries of the universe are very encouraging to me and fuel my imagination. There's always more to discover!
  —Gabrielle, 28, social services worker

How do you make decisions about what you believe and about the practices you'll pursue?

- Through your head?

  For most of my life, "faith" was in direct opposition to my preferences for logic and clarity. Many of my early spiritual experiences involved opinions, not beliefs. Opinions often shift—they are influenced by emotions and experiences. Beliefs should be deeper than that. One should base beliefs on well-developed frameworks that bear up under logical examination. I have to know not just what I believe, but why.
  —Barry, 61, executive

- Through your heart?

  For me, faith is an intersection between God and us, and between me and others. Often, I'm prompted to carry out a certain deed on behalf of others, only to find out later how well my deed matched their need. You can't get me to argue about the existence of God—my faith obviously brings results. As I see it, I entered into a covenant with God long ago and it's an ongoing force in my life. When I respond to what God asks of me, I can live through whatever comes my way.
  —Noel, 68, retired corporate trainer

This is the essence of personality type: how we take in information and how we make decisions, and information-gathering and decision-making are also key processes for exploring how and why we pursue spirituality. Carl Jung developed the theory of psychological types. You might be more familiar with Jung's theory through Isabel Myers's work, the Myers-Briggs Type Indicator® tool, which is one of the most widely-used personality instruments for self-awareness in the world.

Jung, the son of a minister, was intensely interested in spiritual matters. A sign over the doorway of his home read, "Seek or not, God is there." He developed his theory of personality type, the subject of this chapter, as a tool for better understanding ourselves, allowing us to deepen our spiritual side. Melding spirituality and psychological type is natural. *Psyche* (the root of the word *psychology*) comes from the Greek word for "spirit" or "soul." *Soul* as defined in the dictionary refers to the intangible part of us, or our spirit. Thus, to tap into our spiritual side through the psyche is to combine two intellectual disciplines, psychology and theology, about intangible concepts made tangible by looking at their expression in our everyday behavior.

Jung theorized that we have natural preferences for how we
- gain energy (through Extraversion or Introversion);
- take in information (through Sensing or Intuition);
- make decisions (through Thinking or Feeling);
- approach life (through Judging or Perceiving).

These preferences are innate but can be influenced by our families, education, culture, and so on.

Similar to these psychological preferences, we also have physical preferences such as for the hand we write with. Take a moment to sign your name with your non preferred hand in the space below:

What adjectives describe the experience? Awkward? Slow? Sloppy? Hard? Unnatural? Time-consuming? Now write your name with your preferred hand:

Was it easier, more natural? Did it take less concentration, as most people find? Your handedness is innate, as is kicking a ball with your preferred leg or focusing a camera image with your preferred eye. However, with practice, you can learn to use your non preferred hand or leg or eye. And so it is with our personality preferences. We are born into one way of being. That path generally feels more instinctive and typically requires less effort than using the non preferred ways. However, we can improve our abilities with the other preferences through practice.

Type and Spirituality

While infinite varieties of people are found within each of the sixteen psychological types, many similarities are also apparent and provide clues for understanding how each type can best pursue a spiritual path. One of our friends who critiqued part of an early draft of this book commented on his intensive soulwork, "I see from your text that I have once again followed a type path: rather disturbing when one thinks one has simply pursued truth, apparently with reasonable independence and integrity!" Other people who have participated in workshops on the subject reported:

- I understand more why my spiritual practices are different from others—but not wrong!
- I learned that my natural form of soulwork is consistent with my type and can be termed "prayer."
- I want to find out the types of the rest of my family—I have a good feeling that our disputes about spirituality could be aided through the concepts of type.

If you are not familiar with psychological type, the following pages can give you an approximation of your type, but you may wish to read further. Our suggested reading list at the end of the book provides further clarity and other applications of type beyond spirituality.

Extraversion or Introversion: Our Pathway to Energy

In a Nutshell

Extraverts are energized through contact with other people or through engaging in activities.

Introverts are energized through the world of ideas, pulling back from activities to allow time for thought and reflection.

The first of the preference pairings describes how we are energized. Think about the many different activities and environments you encountered during the past week. Some of them probably left you feeling energetic and refreshed, while others were stressful and draining, causing you to seek rest and renewal elsewhere.

To begin exploring whether your preference is for Extraversion (E) or Introversion (I), consider, which way would you have approached the assignment in Jane's story below?

> *I attended a writers' workshop at a retreat center. One evening our leader dismissed the group to work on the assignment of identifying our strengths as writers and our aspirations for the coming year. As an Introvert, I couldn't wait to get to my room—the evening session had covered so much and I was ready to organize my thoughts on paper. I made a little grid of ideas I wanted to consider. What was most on my heart? The next ninety minutes flew by as my pen filled the paper. For me, this quiet time alone on the retreat was the most meaningful segment of the weekend.*
>
> *The next morning, I heard that several of the participants—including the leader—never quite made it to their rooms to journal. Instead, they chose to use each other as sounding boards, tossing out ideas and dreams to allow those listening to give input on the patterns and strengths they saw. At breakfast, they were still bubbling about the insights they had gained through their discussion.*

Jane's preference is for *Introversion*—that is, she gains energy by retreating, taking time to reflect and to process her inner thoughts. Those who stayed together to interact probably preferred *Extraversion*—they were energized by talking through their thoughts with others. Different methods, same results.

Which method would work best for you—off alone or together in discussion? Now consider the following word pairings as you try to determine your own preference for energy:

Extraversion	Introversion
__People and things	__Thoughts and ideas
__Try, then consider	__Consider, then try
__Action	__Reflection
__Breadth, different subjects	__Depth on one subject
__Outer energy	__Inner energy
__Interruptions are stimulating	__Interruptions are distracting
__Focus outside	__Focus inside
__Say what they are thinking	__Keep thoughts to themselves
__Discuss to process ideas	__Introspect to process ideas
__Offer suggestions freely	__Hold suggestions until clear

A Natural Environment for Extraverted Soulwork

If Extraverted types could design their own atmosphere for soulwork, they would include people, action, and variety; they gain energy from the world around them. Extraverted types learn best by talking through spiritual matters and joining with others for worship, study, or service activities. They see God or the spiritual through their own actions and the words and deeds of others.

If Extraverted types are part of silent environments, attend meetings or services with long pauses for meditation, or are required to sit still or focus on one idea for too long, they might conclude that they struggle spiritually.

A Natural Environment for Introverted Soulwork

Solitude, introspection, and privacy for personal reflection are key to spirituality for Introverted types. They gain energy in the world of ideas. Introverted types learn best through study, reading, contemplation, or one-to-one conversations. They may not even pray aloud or discuss their soulwork with close friends.

If Introverted types spend too much time in group discussion, participating in active learning experiences, or are asked to share deep thoughts too freely, they might mistakenly conclude that they struggle spiritually.

Sensing or Intuition: Our Pathway to Discovery

In a Nutshell
Sensing types pay attention to what they perceive through their five senses—seeing, hearing, touching, smelling, and tasting.

Intuitive types pay attention to what might be described as their sixth sense—the unseen world of meanings, inferences, hunches, insights, and connections.

Information surrounds us every day of our lives—sights, sounds, conversations, readings, events, changes in the weather, and the products of our imaginations. Our perceiving processes involve sorting through all of this data. We naturally filter the things to which we pay attention. None of us can process it all. There are two ways to perceive, either Sensing (S) or using Intuition (N).*

How might you have reacted to the following experience?

> *I joined a cancer support group that was recommended by a friend. The first meeting was filled with concrete tips on information-gathering, dealing with chemotherapy, and examples of how others had dealt with decisions about cancer care. Then at the end of the session our leader handed each of us a rock. "Imagine that the weight of this stone is the weight of your personal sorrows and concerns. They weigh on your soul just as this rock weighs down your hand. Let's take a moment to ponder that weight in silence and consider the effect of the burdens we carry. Then as you leave, drop your rock into the basket by the door. Leave your fears about cancer here as well, taking with you only the proactive plan you've developed tonight."*
>
> *Out in the hall, I was amazed to see that some of the participants had tears in their eyes as a result of the closing exercise, saying that they were able to let go of their anxieties as they let go of the rock. This did nothing for me; the rock was a rock—gray, cold, and hard. I felt just as burdened as before. I tried not to make too much of my reaction, but I wondered why I was affected so differently when the others seemed to have shared a meaningful experience.*
>
> —Jon, 54, a retail manager

Jon has a preference for Sensing—relying on information that is provided by the five senses. Many of those who found meaning and help in the stone exercise probably had preferences for Intuition—going beyond the facts that provide a starting point for using the imagination and making connections.

Which word list on the next page resonates most with you?

---

*"N" is used for Intuition because "I" is used to denote Introversion.

Sensing	Intuition
__Five senses	__Sixth sense
__Common sense	__Insight
__Accuracy	__Creativity
__Past experience	__Inspiration
__Real world	__Unseen world
__Current reality	__Future potential
__Immediacy, concreteness	__Anticipation
__Master, then apply skills	__Learn new skills, then innovate
__Simplicity, clarity	__Complexity
__What experiences offer people	__What possibilities offer people

A Natural Spiritual Environment for Sensing Types

If Sensing types could design their own spiritual setting, it might be filled with tangible evidence that supports their values and principles, suggestions for activities and tasks, methods for study and prayer, the examples of others who have found soulwork meaningful, and opportunities to serve in practical ways. Soulwork, they might say, should make a difference in the here and now.

Some Sensing types struggle if asked to believe too many assumptions without good facts or evidence. Their preference for concreteness can make them feel somewhat out of place in many spiritual communities, where often the emphasis is on accepting on faith what cannot be proved.

A Natural Spiritual Environment for Intuitive Types

If Intuitive types could design an atmosphere for soulwork, they might fill it with symbols, imagery, the creative, the artistic, or the poetic—spurs to the imagination that provide inspiration. Learning often comes through synchronistic interactions among ideas, people, and the environment. Change and innovation tend to enrich their spirituality.

Intuitive types might struggle in environments with fixed routines, narrow interpretations, or defined methods for soulwork that leave little room for innovation. If their soulwork becomes too familiar, their minds may wander or their attention may be captured elsewhere, leaving them to feel unspiritual.

Thinking or Feeling: Our Pathway to Decisions

In a Nutshell

Thinking types base their decisions on impartial criteria—cause-effect reasoning, constant principles or truths, and logical analysis.

Feeling types consider the impact of their decisions on people—their needs and those of others, the values to be served, and circumstantial or community variables.

We all use our perceiving process, either Sensing or Intuition, to gather information. We also need to sort through that information and act on it. To do so, we operate out of our preference for Thinking (T) or Feeling (F). Both approaches are rational decision-making processes; however, only one can be termed "logical," while the other might be described as "values-centered." Think how often these styles play out in our day-to-day conversations—"I *think* we should do this." And "I *feel* the same way!"

Our decision-making style has a profound impact on how we evaluate experiences, define our beliefs, and view the actions of others. Consider how you might react in this situation Sandra describes:

> In a seminar on the soul at work, our instructor asked us to ponder what our lifework might be. As music played softly in the background, several members of the class jotted down their thoughts while I simply closed my eyes.
>
> The discussion that followed impressed me with the heartfelt reflections about purpose and fulfillment. One person mentioned a value his lifework needed to fulfill. Another mentioned striving toward a change she hoped to bring about in employee-employer relationships. As the stories and affirmations about our lifework continued, the man next to me interjected, "I'm beginning to wonder about the kind of planet I landed on tonight. As I pondered my lifework, I concluded that I don't need to analyze all of this other stuff. I like my work and I'm good at it. My corporation serves a useful purpose, we've created products that fill a need—why look beyond the work I am doing right now?"

Many class participants were looking to define their life work in terms of the impact they could have on other people or on society, perhaps out of their preference for Feeling. The last speaker had examined his work through a logical framework of usefulness and productivity, a more Thinking process.

Which of the words in the pairings below seem to fit your decision-making style?

Thinking	Feeling
__Easily sort ideas about data and things	__Easily sort ideas about people
__Acknowledge differences	__Acknowledge common ground
__Critique	__Appreciate
__Logical, analytical	__Harmonious, personal
__Reasons	__Values
__Head knowledge	__Heart knowledge
__Fair but firm	__Empathize, make exceptions
__Analyze	__Sympathize
__Content of message	__Impact of message
__Convince through impartiality	__Convince through personal meaning

A Natural Environment for Thinking Soulwork

If Thinking types could design their atmosphere for soulwork, they would start with the intellect, searching for universal principles and sacred truths. Their skepticism often precedes conviction. Learning occurs through debate and dialogue, logical explanations of issues, categorizing practices and beliefs, and working to establish standards and structures. They may discount or distrust the emotional aspects of spirituality.

If Thinking types find themselves in atmospheres that emphasize soulwork through personal encounters or relationships with their Creator, they may consider themselves inadequate if they lack these spiritual experiences. They may also struggle unless others let them probe and question—a form of soulwork that feels threatening to some people.

A Natural Environment for Feeling Soulwork

If Feeling types could design their own atmosphere for soulwork, they would start with the heart, searching for personal meaning and values. Relationships with others are often key to their spirituality. Learning occurs through direct acts of service and in trying to explain the motivations, inspirations, and experiences of others. They also want compassionate environments that put people and their needs first.

If Feeling types find themselves in atmospheres that enforce rules without love, require logical, objective rationale for what they believe, or offer an impersonal approach to soulwork, they may struggle spiritually.

Judging or Perceiving: Our Pathway to Soulwork

In a Nutshell

Judging types like to order their lives—plan ahead, wrap things up, and accomplish set goals.

Perceiving types like to live life as it unfolds—keep their options open and enjoy what comes along.

People tend to approach life in one of two ways: Judging (J) types like to plan their work and work their plan, soulwork included; Perceiving (P) types prefer to go with the flow, remaining open to soulwork as opportunities arise.

Where do you place yourself in this story?

> *When my spouse suggested a daily family time to connect with each other, it seemed like a wonderful idea—a planned activity, a chance for everyone to report on their day, a question to ponder—perhaps ten or fifteen minutes after dinner. At first, I shared the enthusiasm for these times, but after a while I began to feel locked in and duty-bound. Instead of enriched, I felt smothered, dreading the daily dinner "ritual."*
>
> *My spouse, who really enjoyed this time, was upset when I said I preferred not to continue. For a long time, I felt guilty about backing out and canceling the routine. I wondered how one of us could find these moments so meaningful and the other find the structure and predictability so deadening.*
>
> —Cynthia, 42, career counselor

Our storyteller prefers the Perceiving process, approaching life as it comes and finding richness and joy in spontaneity. The spouse took a more Judging approach, enjoying the planning of their family time. Consider your own preference in the following word pairings:

Judging	Perceiving
__Planned events	__Serendipitous events
__Work before play	__Work and play coexist
__Stress reduced by planning ahead	__Stress reduced by identifying contingencies
__Enjoy making the decision	__Enjoy gathering information
__Goal-oriented	__Discovery-oriented
__Tasks in order	__Several tasks at random
__Settled and decided	__Open to late-breaking information
__Choose one option, then explore	__Explore many options, then choose
__Select the best experience	__Experience as much as possible
__Settled, orderly	__In the moment

A Natural Environment for Judging Soulwork

If Judging types could design their atmosphere for soulwork, the key elements might be discipline, organization, and schedule. They might develop regular routines for their devotional practices, using benchmarks for recording progress and accomplishments. Learning often occurs through structured exercises or regular classes.

If Judging types are in environments where things don't start and end on time, there is little drive to closure, others aren't prepared, or stated goals aren't accomplished, their frustrations may cause them to lose their desire for soulwork.

A Natural Environment for Perceiving Soulwork

If Perceiving types could design their atmosphere for soulwork, it would be flexible, full of options, stocked with resources, and able to adapt time frames to the needs of people or circumstances. Learning comes from departures as much as from staying on task, being open to more facts and possibilities, and experiencing as many avenues for soulwork as possible when opportunities arise.

If Perceiving types are corralled in environments that are too structured, they may either feel inadequate or concerned that they lack the discipline others say they need to grow spiritually. They often find that systematic spiritual disciplines (which permeate literature on prayer and other writings on enriching one's soulwork) threaten to dampen their chances of finding the sacred as they go about experiencing life.

Your Type Preferences

These eight preferences combine to describe sixteen different psychological types. Because you might find it interesting and because our writing comes from who we are—our personality—Sandra's preferences are for Extraversion, Intuition, Feeling, and Perceiving, more easily written as the type ENFP. Jane's preferences are for Introversion, Intuition, Feeling, and Judging, more easily written as the type INFJ. For brevity, the preferences are known by the first letter in the word. (The "N," however, stands for Intuition, because "I" was used for Introversion.) You can record your four-letter type in the spaces below:

_____	_____	_____	_____
E or I	S or N	T or F	J or P

A Few Observations about Type

While we want to emphasize that type is only one tool for soulwork, it provides key insights for many people as they work to enrich their spiritual journey. However please note the following:

- Personality type is not prescriptive. It is a tool for describing recognizable distinctions between people.
- Personality type is not a pigeonhole. Human behavior is much too complex to be described through a single framework. In addition, infinite diversity exists among human beings and within each of the sixteen psychological types. People with the same type will share some common characteristics, but each will have many unique characteristics of his or her own.
- Personality type is not deterministic. While Jung believed that you are born a certain type (think of the differences in siblings you know!), you are also born with a free will that gives you latitude for your behavior. You also have your own particular life circumstances that shape the expression of your type.

- Personality type offers little information about your particular skills, competencies, abilities, or knowledge base.
- Personality type is not an excuse for certain behaviors or for avoiding certain tasks.
- Personality type is not about putting barriers in the way of your personal or spiritual growth.

For this book, type is a tool, not the answer, for understanding yourself and learning how to make your spiritual life more meaningful. As you look to use this book to strengthen your soulwork, keep the following in mind:

- Type is a way to understand yourself in general, not in specifics. For advice about the most natural paths to soulwork for people of your type, read the chapter about your type. But then read the other chapters to understand similarities, differences, and new paths for enrichment.
- Type is a logical framework for explaining some of the consistencies of human behavior. As such, for spirituality it can improve communication, emphasize the value of diversity, identify potential conflicts, and offer an appropriate language to deal with emotional or stressful issues.
- Finally, type is a dynamic theory, not a method for placing people in unchanging boxes. As the next chapter describes in detail, type can be used to explore strategies for growth and development over the span of life, as well as help you anticipate your responses when life is difficult.

CHAPTER TWO

GROWING TOWARD WHOLENESS AND MEANING

Before we examine the eight main spiritual paths in the chapters that follow, we first want to be very clear about our main findings in our discussions with people of every personality type. Personality type points to a natural path for finding enriching practices for prayer, worship, service, and other forms of soulwork that draw us closer to God. In general, people whose natural paths were honored in their early faith experiences reported that religion or spirituality had always been important to them. Those whose early experiences were very different from their natural paths often struggled to fit in or to believe.

However, our *natural* path is just the starting place for a lifelong spiritual journey. It can only take us so far. As we mature, as our questions grow bigger, as our yearning for meaning and purpose increases, often the paths of other personality types add richness, freshness, and new significance to soulwork.

The theory of *type dynamics* acts as a guide for where to explore and what to expect on the lifelong spiritual journey because type is more than just your four letters—it is also a theory about growing toward wholeness and adding meaning to your life. Herein lies the value of type dynamics in pursuing soulwork. To understand the implications of type theory, consider for now just the two middle letters of your type—S or N, T or F. These four preferences—Sensing or Intuition, Thinking or Feeling—describe how we *function*. The order in which you learn to use these functions also says something about your spirituality.

Chart 2.1 below shows the sixteen MBTI® types and the typical order of function preferences for each—dominant, auxiliary, "third," and inferior. Find your type on the chart so that you can refer to it throughout the next sections.

2.1 MBTI® Type and Order of Function Preferences

ISTJ	ISFJ	INFJ	INTJ
1. Sensing	1. Sensing	1. Intuition	1. Intuition
2. Thinking	2. Feeling	2. Feeling	2. Thinking
3. Feeling	3. Thinking	3. Thinking	3. Feeling
4. Intuition	4. Intuition	4. Sensing	4. Sensing
ISTP	**ISFP**	**INFP**	**INTP**
1. Thinking	1. Feeling	1. Feeling	1. Thinking
2. Sensing	2. Sensing	2. Intuition	2. Intuition
3. Intuition	3. Intuition	3. Sensing	3. Sensing
4. Feeling	4. Thinking	4. Thinking	4. Feeling
ESTP	**ESFP**	**ENFP**	**ENTP**
1. Sensing	1. Sensing	1. Intuition	1. Intuition
2. Thinking	2. Feeling	2. Feeling	2. Thinking
3. Feeling	3. Thinking	3. Thinking	3. Feeling
4. Intuition	4. Intuition	4. Sensing	4. Sensing
ESTJ	**ESFJ**	**ENFJ**	**ENTJ**
1. Thinking	1. Feeling	1. Feeling	1. Thinking
2. Sensing	2. Sensing	2. Intuition	2. Intuition
3. Intuition	3. Intuition	3. Sensing	3. Sensing
4. Feeling	4. Thinking	4. Thinking	4. Feeling

The Role of the Dominant Function

Each of us has a dominant function, the function listed first in the chart on page 37. People use their dominant preference first in most situations and it develops earliest in life. Most people we interviewed agree that it points to their natural spiritual path.

Consider your childhood in view of your dominant function as indicated in the chart on page 37:

- Many dominant *Sensing types* were described as sensible or matter-of-fact youngsters.
- Many dominant *Intuitive types* were described as imaginative or creative children.
- Many dominant *Thinking types* were described as inquisitive kids, full of questions, frequently asking, "Why?"
- Many dominant *Feeling types* were described as empathetic children, considerate of the feelings of others and concerned that everyone be included.

To describe how people with the various dominant functions approach soulwork, the following chapters of *SoulTypes* are divided into two sections. Part 2 describes Sensing and Intuitive spirituality, the two functions that describe how we take in information. Part 3 describes Thinking and Feeling spirituality, the two functions that describe how we make decisions. Each section starts with exercises and stories that reflect the contrasting spiritual paths described in that section.

The Role of Extraversion and Introversion

Within each section of the chapter, you will find descriptions of the Extraverted and Introverted spiritual paths—for example, Extraverted Sensing (chapter 3) and Introverted Sensing (chapter 4). Your preference for Extraversion or Introversion tells the *orientation* of your dominant function. Extraverts show their dominant function to the outer world of people and activities. Introverts use their dominant function in the inner world—the life of the mind. Jane as an INFJ, for example, processes her ideas internally, generating possibilities and connections on her own. *Introverted* Intuition is the orientation of her dominant function. In contrast, Sandra as an ENFP processes aloud with others, getting her ideas from the world at large, what she sees and what others say. *Extraverted* Intuition is the orientation of her dominant function.

SoulTypes has separate chapters on the Extraverted and Introverted forms of Sensing, Intuition, Thinking, and Feeling. These illustrate the eight profoundly different natural paths people pursue for prayer, worship, and other spiritual practices.

The Role of the Auxiliary Function

Complementing each type's natural element and dominant function are the gifts of the *auxiliary* function, the second one listed for your type in the chart on page 37. Together, the dominant and auxiliary make up the two middle letters of your type code. Without a well-developed auxiliary function, people lack balance.*

If your dominant function is one of the perceiving funtions: *Sensing or* *Intuition*	then your auxiliary function is one of the judging functions: *Thinking or* *Feeling.* This function enables you to act on all of the information your dominant function gathers.
If your dominant function is one of the judging functions: *Thinking or* *Feeling*	then your auxiliary function is one of the perceiving functions: *Sensing or* *Intuition.* This function gives you information for the decision-making process of your dominant function.

After the dominant function, the auxiliary function is the next to develop in life. By young adulthood, most people are able to use this function efficiently, allowing them to gather information and to make decisions.

---

*S and N, Sensing and Intuition, are the Perceiving functions; T and F, Thinking and Feeling, are the Judging functions. The last letter in your type code points to the function you use in the outer world, which is the dominant function for Extraverts and the auxiliary function for Introverts. Your dominant function is either a Perceiving one (S or N) or a Judging one (T or F).

The *orientation* of the auxiliary function is opposite that of the dominant function. For example, since Jane's dominant function, Intuition, is *Introverted*, then her auxiliary function, Feeling, is *Extraverted*. In order to understand her feelings and the effects of a situation on people, Jane often finds it helpful to talk things through with others or engage in activities to gain new perspectives. As we worked on this book, Jane spent considerable time interviewing people to understand their soulwork and determine what might be included in these pages.

Sandra's dominant function, Intuition, is *Extraverted*, so the orientation of her auxiliary function, Feeling, is *Introverted*. Sandra often needs time by herself to consider exactly how she feels about a situation. In writing this book, Sandra reflected alone on what might be most helpful for others and how to make our treatment of the subject as affirming to each type as possible.

The Third Function

So far we have explained the middle letters of your type. However, the letters that *are not* present in your four-letter type influence you as well. For example, if your middle letters are NF, then the "missing" functions S and T also play an active part in your type.

Type theory suggests that during the first half of life, we operate mostly through our dominant and auxiliary functions. This makes sense if you consider that the first half of life is about separating from our families of origin, establishing our careers, building our primary relationships, and perhaps becoming parents. Success in these endeavors often comes through operating out of our most natural functions.

However, as we move toward the second half of life, the focus changes. Perhaps we experience a vague yearning for more.

"Is this all there is to life?"

"I can't understand . . ."

"I've been successful, but what have I really achieved?"

Carl Jung held that our first two functions are not enough to bring fulfillment in life—we must learn to access our non preferred processes. He stated it thus: "We cannot live in the afternoon of life according to the program of life's morning—for what . . . in the morning was true will at evening have become a lie."[1]

For many people, the two missing functions come into play at this time of life. Generally, we begin to access our third function next, and that's why it's referred to as the third function. Not as much is known about the third function. Carl Jung wrote that, for most of us, this function is sometimes conscious, sometimes unconscious. This third function is more difficult for us to access and for most people is not as well developed as the dominant and auxiliary functions.

Whereas we describe the first, second, and fourth function (see below) in terms of Extraversion and Introversion, we cannot say the same about the third function. Some type practitioners say that the third function can be either Extraverted or Introverted at different times. However, we do know that:

- Sensing, the gift of seeing what is, is the third function for ENTJs, ENFJs, INFPs and INTPs. These types tend to be more adept at perceiving through their auxiliary Intuition function. However, taking a common-sense approach to life, being aware of facts and specifics, is occasionally required. For these four types, developing their third function of Sensing can help them back up their Intuitive insights with the necessary details.

- Intuition, the gift of seeing what could be, is the third function for ESTJs, ESFJs, ISTPs, and ISFPs. These types tend to be more adept at perceiving through their auxiliary Sensing function. At times, however, adding insight and inspiration can be useful. For these four types, developing their third function of Intuition can help them enlarge their view of reality, value the big picture, and be open to new ways of doing things.

- Thinking, the gift of logic and clarity, is the third function for ESFPs, ENFPs, ISFJs, and INFJs. These types tend to be more adept at making decisions through their auxiliary Feeling function. However, by developing their third function, Thinking, they may find it easier to debate and logically support their viewpoints, adding objectivity to their decision-making process.

- Feeling, the gift of understanding and appreciating the values and viewpoints of others, is the third function for ESTPs, ENTPs, ISTJs, and INTJs. These types tend to be more adept at making decisions through their auxiliary Thinking function. At times, however, focusing on subjective values or analyzing the impact on people of different alternatives can be useful. For these four types, developing their third function, Feeling, can often add more persuasive language and soften their more tough-minded decision-making style.

How people use their third function in soulwork varies greatly. Although we don't address it in the chapters that focus on each spiritual path, you can explore ideas about using the third function in soulwork by identifying it in the chart on page 37 and looking at the summary pages for Sensing, Intuitive, Thinking, or Feeling spirituality, whichever is the third function for your type.

The Fourth or Inferior Function

Finally there is the fourth function, often known as the *inferior function*, which typically develops last, at midlife and beyond. For most people, their inferior function is the opposite of their dominant and by far the most difficult to learn to use effectively. It is hard to discern the facts and the possibilities (Sensing and Intuition) at the same time. It is hard to be objective and subjective (Thinking and Feeling) at the same time. This means that t he inferior function, even more unconscious and undeveloped than the third function, can be a blind spot and a source of many problems for us:

- Dominant Sensing types (ISTJ, ISFJ, ESTP, ESFP), so versed in identifying *what is*, may have difficulty accessing what *could be*—the realm of their inferior *Intuitive* function.
- Dominant Intuitive types (INFJ, INTJ, ENFP, ENTP), so adept in using their imagination and developing new insights, may struggle in dealing with day-to-day details or realism—the realm of their inferior *Sensing* function.
- Dominant Thinking types (ISTP, INTP, ESTJ, ENTJ), with their ease at being objective and analytical, may struggle with interpersonal matters where subjectivity and harmony are valued—the realm of their inferior *Feeling* function.
- Dominant Feeling types (ISFP, INFP, ESFJ, ENFJ), acutely aware of the impact of events and ideas on themselves and others, may find it difficult to deal objectively with tough issues—the realm of their inferior *Thinking* function.

The pages devoted to your specific personality type provide information on ways you might struggle with your inferior function and possible spiritual helps for those times when life is difficult.

However, while often being a source of trouble, the inferior function also adds richness and many rewards to the second half of life. New vistas for soulwork are available for those who tap this fourth function.

As a dominant Extraverted Feeling type, I had one use for my boat—parties! For me, the more people, the better. I'd have twenty on the boat with me and twenty more on shore waiting for the next round. I skippered, kept the buffet table full and the soda flowing, in short, being the life of the party.

Last year, though, something changed for me. The boat became a means of getting away from people in order to think. The lapping of the water and the feel of the breeze were all but unnoticeable when I was surrounded by dozens of people. Sometimes I stop the engines and drift in silence as my mind ponders a decision. My inferior Introverted Thinking now can provide the peace and wisdom I used to look for from others.

—Keith, 68, retired minister

While the dominant function is often the initial spark for pursuing spirituality, some of the deepest spiritual growth is fed through this inferior function. Perhaps this is because few things that are extremely important to us come easily. In addition, as long as we are using our dominant function, most of us are in control of ourselves and the processes we are pursuing. When we enter the domain of the inferior function, few of us can effectively control the process. We need to be more deliberate, more disciplined to use this fourth function. For many of us, this is where God can get our attention—we stop trying to control and are more open to the Creator.

At the end of the description of each type's spiritual path (for example, see page 60) are stories about how people found rich spiritual practices by using their inferior function. In fact, at many retreats we have conducted, as people examine the role their fourth function plays in prayer and worship, they exclaim, "Who says this is the 'inferior' function? It's the pathway to experiences I didn't know were possible when I was younger."

As you continue through *SoulTypes*, remember that, while some spiritual pursuits may be labeled as more Sensing, Intuitive, Thinking, or Feeling, all of us can benefit from operating outside of our normal ways. However, it helps to know that this is what we are doing.

How to Use This Book

To chart the most meaningful spiritual path for you, personally, at this stage in your life, we suggest that you might approach *SoulTypes* in the following way:

- Identify your dominant function, then start by engaging in the introductory exercise that includes it, either Sensing and Intuition (page 46) or Thinking and Feeling (page 142).

- Read the chapter for your natural spiritual path. Try what fits, take what you want, leave the rest.

Keep in mind that, while your natural path is either Extraverted or Introverted, because one of your first two functions is Extraverted and one is Introverted, you need both outer and inner approaches to soulwork. You will find suggestions for using your second function, the one that balances the dominant function, in the pages on your individual type. This does not mean that if you are Introverted you must join an organized spiritual community or if you are Extraverted you must discipline yourself for extended periods of solitude. It simply means that Extraverts will flourish by finding some time for reflection and Introverts will flourish by finding at least a few like-minded souls as companions on their spiritual journey.

Following the exploration of the first two functions, the next step is exploring the spiritual path opposite your natural path—the path of your inferior function. Look at the chapter for your opposite type to gain a real sense of the differences between your own dominant and inferior functions. While the chapter on your type has examples of how some people use their inferior function, you may want to observe the spirituality of people whose preferences are opposite from yours—or talk with them—to gain vivid images of the gifts of their natural soulwork.

In families or relationships, you might use these pages to
- become aware of the different psychological types of your family members and their natural avenues for soulwork;
- look through the chapters to find common ground for spirituality;
- decide where you can support each other—what practices and opportunities does each person need the chance to pursue?
- encourage each other to try new spiritual practices to enrich the journey and for spiritual development.

And finally, for those of you who are spiritual directors or leaders, we ask you to reconsider any "shoulds" and "oughts" through the lens of type. What would honor *all* types, or at least respectfully acknowledge type differences?

PART TWO

Sensing and Intuitive Spirituality

INTRODUCTION:
A SENSORY EXERCISE

Before you read further, try the following soulwork exercise:

Go outside, take a walk, find something in nature, and spend five minutes concentrating on present-moment experiences. Use your senses, not metaphors or connections, to find the spiritual in the here and now. Write down your observations and your thoughts about how the experience is spiritual in the space below.

At many of our spiritual retreats, we ask *everyone* to participate in this exercise. Why? Because all too often the Intuitive form of spirituality, with its mysticism, mystery, and concentration on the unseen, is held up as the "right" way to be spiritual (remember the brainwave experiments described on page 14?). This exercise taps into the Sensing side of all of us.

The following sample responses to this exercise are from a retreat we facilitated on a gorgeous fall day. The grounds of the retreat center allowed participants to meander through orchards, meadows, woods, and gardens.

Responses from Sensing Participants

How easy it is to find the spiritual in nature!
Whispering sounds of grass and trees
Sweet, clean smell of fermenting apples dropped to the ground
Textures of birch bark beside me, a fallen feather, a magenta clover
Bark, so thick at one end, transparent at the other
As I lie under a balsam, I sense the earth, the tree, the change of year
  in the field. Nature is God.

I observed three dandelions. Yellow . . . three-fourths-inch in diameter, dozens of tiny petals, all turned toward the sun. So perfect, yet considered a weed. As I watched, bees stopped to collect nectar from my flowers. Dandelions have a life purpose: to provide food for bees.

Responses from Intuitive Participants

Initially I noticed someone else scribbling away and wondered, "What is he spending so much time on?" I just wanted to sit, take in everything. Recording details is hard. I see the whole, not the specifics. I gaze at a small evergreen, nearly aqua in color . . . okay, is there anything else to see in this tree? It's so hard to stay in the present—one detail is like a gateway to "other." I should touch the tree, use another sense . . . make a note to do that.

What an effort to stay in my senses. "I want to go further, interpret, I need to remind myself to get back to seeing and touching. I try to focus on petunias but soon catch myself daydreaming. One Sensing thought leads to ninety-nine Intuitive thoughts. I hit the wall, but pushed myself to try again. I can't say this is inspiring . . . more intriguing . . . there's a real world out there! Petunias have different leaf colors and textures. There's a relaxation in using my senses. Still, I feel urged to get back to important things. What is the point of all this?

Rotting tree with a nail . . . but still leaves grow, new branches, signs of life. I flip into thoughts of Jesus and the cross. I pull back to details . . . three bird houses . . . Jesus and the two thieves. A rock at the base of the tree . . . the stone rolled away at the tomb. I should touch the tree, try to stay with the moment, but I'm too comfortable. Red berries . . . Jesus' blood. Loose branch . . . we hang like that, precarious. I can't see beyond the metaphors!!!

We ask the Intuitive participants to tell about their experiences first. As the above samples show, they are often a disgruntled lot. "What was the point?" "Can we get on to something else?" "The only benefit of details is the connections that transpire."

That disgruntlement turns to amazement as the Sensing participants share the richness of their experiences. "What *are* we missing in life?" the Intuitive types ask.

Come learn about the richness of the Sensing and Intuitive spiritual journeys in the pages that follow. Chapters 3 and 4 describe the spiritual paths of Extraverted and Introverted Sensing types. Chapters 5 and 6 explore the characteristics of Extraverted and Introverted Intuitives' spiritual paths.

The Paths of Sensing Spirituality

The year's at the spring
And day's at the morn;
Morning's at seven;
The hillside's dew-pearled;
The lark's on the wing;
The snail's on the thorn:
God's in his heaven—
All's right with the world.[1]
—*Robert Browning*

Sensing types find satisfying soulwork through

- living the spiritual life with an emphasis on what's happening in the here and now;
- enjoying the gifts of being alive, the delights of this world;
- appreciating the beauty of nature and creation, the joys of "what is";
- seeing tangible applications for the day-to-day real world, practical works and needs;
- learning in an orderly, step-by-step fashion about facts, history, or methods of spirituality;
- observing concrete examples of what has worked for others;
- commemorating spiritual traditions and events.

Preferred Extraverted Sensing Soulwork (Ch. 3: ESTP and ESFP)	Preferred Introverted Sensing Soulwork (Ch. 4: ISTJ and ISFJ)
• Prayer/meditation in the moment, as an event, blessing or need occurs	• Prayer/meditation through consistent, private conversation with God
• Soulwork through activities, nature, being with others	• Soulwork through an appreciation of the continuity of traditions and creeds
• Spontaneous spiritual life, happiness in the midst of the celebration of life	• Sequential, structured spiritual life, typically with set times or routines
• Service through action to solve immediate problems concerning people, organizations, natural world	• Service, often behind the scenes, organizing to meet current needs

Suggestions for Sensing Spirituality

1. Prepare a special place for your soulwork—perhaps your favorite easy chair, a corner of a room, a beautiful walking route, or a bench by a local pond. Make sure that you can be there frequently. If it is a spot in your home, what might you do to make it more welcoming? Add a flower vase? Stock it with special mementos? Have music nearby? Clarify with others that this space and time is for you and your soulwork. Ask for their support in not disturbing you.

2. What could you add to soulwork that would engage your senses? If you write, try brightly colored pens or one that is superbly smooth. Buy a special notebook for journaling. Purchase a distinctive candle. Find a favorite kind of coffee or tea and save it for your reflective moments. Get that bicycle, set of skis, or walking shoes you have always wanted, if that will draw you more often to the work of your soul.

3. For the discipline of simplicity: Examine your life to determine what things bring joy. What things take away joy? Many Sensing types discover that the complexities of modern life separate them from the things that bring them closest to their soul. What simple pleasures are you missing or no longer able to do? How can you bring those pleasures back into your life?

4. For the discipline of celebration: Take time to mark the milestones of your life with special festivity—add candles to the dinner table, call a good friend for a walk, take a special photograph to commemorate an event, give a small dinner party, treat yourself to an afternoon at a place that is sacred to you. Besides birthdays or anniversaries, you could celebrate a job well done, the reaching of a specific goal for soulwork, or the gift of a beautiful day.

5. Record several of the favorite and familiar songs that speak to your soul onto one tape or CD so that you can have uninterrupted music for soulwork.

6. *Sensing* soulwork includes tangible acts of help or service to others or projects. At the end of the day, pause to reflect on or write down all of the tasks you have completed or the help you have been able to give to other people. Be thankful that you *see* what needs to be done.

7. Think of someone whose spirituality you would like to emulate. How is your spirituality like and not like theirs? What kinds of

soulwork do they practice? Which practices appeal to you? How can you add these practices to your own life?

8. Consider forming a small group. Decide together your plans for study, activities, or service opportunities to tackle together. Set up expectations and determine a schedule so that the group can remain together for a few months or longer.

9. Reinvestigate your spiritual history, roots, or rituals. Look at the creeds, prayers, or other components of the spiritual tradition you embrace. Which ones might you add to your current soulwork? Which ones could be refreshed? Which ones could be replaced to make time for something more meaningful to you?

10. Keep a written record of your concerns for yourself and others—the requests you offer in prayer or the situations about which you pray or meditate. Look back periodically to see which have changed for the better and rejoice. Which ones are still issues? What might be their spiritual lessons for you?

Extraverted Sensing Soulwork

1. For the discipline of prayer: Think of a habit you would like to change, an attitude you would like to improve, or someone you'd like to help or who needs prayer. Come up with a *very* short phrase that captures your request or petition. Examples might be:

Teach me patience   Help me appreciate what I have
Guide my actions in service   Bring strength/peace/love to ___

Then, let the activities of the day bring your prayer to mind—when the phone rings, as you perform your daily tasks, while dropping off to sleep. You might keep the same prayer for a few days or a few months. If you begin to forget to bring the prayer to mind, consider whether it is time to change it.

2. For the discipline of study: Notice the wonders of the natural world. Spend most of your time simply appreciating the delightful feel of water, the wonder of migrating birds, the miracle that flowers actually bloom, the sounds of rustling leaves when the city is still enough for you to hear. Then consider what new spiritual information these observations could have for you. What might they mean for you? How might you apply lessons from nature to your life?

3. Turn your refrigerator, bulletin board, or scrapbook into a place to record your blessings. Add pictures of friends and families, tickets from events, particularly meaningful greeting cards, or copies of expressive poems or sayings. As occasional soulwork, gaze at or page through these reminders and offer thanks.

4. Find a friend (or two or three) who enjoys your favorite activity. Brainstorm how you might engage in the activity more regularly together. As you golf, walk, fish, work on crafts, cook, stargaze, garden, and so on, be aware of your sense of gratitude for what God provides.

Introverted Sensing Soulwork

1. For the discipline of prayer: Sometimes our most effective praises are for the little things in life. Write a litany of praise in your own style, give thanks for the simple things. You might look to the poetry of Emily Dickinson, e. e. cummings, or the Hebrew Psalms for examples of thanksgiving over the wonders of *this* life.

2. For the discipline of study: Think of a person you love and admire or an activity you enjoy and journal about the following:
   • How do I see God in this person or feel spiritual in this activity?
   • What gifts did God give to this person? Or, what gifts come to me through this activity?
   • What special times have we shared?
   • How has this person or activity enriched my life?
   Pause to be thankful for this person or activity.
   You might also use these questions as you think about a person you struggle to like or an activity that you dislike but in which you must occasionally participate.

3. Go to a favorite spot, either outdoors or indoors, where you feel in touch with your soul. Look and listen for specific signs of God's love, beauty, wisdom, and goodness. How has God been revealed in the events of your life? In its history? You may wish to write down your praises to God.

4. Consider framing a poem, favorite saying, or passage from your sacred readings. Keep it on your desk or by your bedside as a reminder for your soulwork.

CHAPTER THREE

EXTRAVERTED
SENSING:

The Active Spiritual Path

Extraverted Sensing Spirituality
ESTP, ESFP

*Appreciating and engaging fully in the life given to us,
connecting soulwork with the recreational, social,
intellectual, and vocational parts of us.*

At one of our seminars, a man whose dominant function is Intuition said, "I don't get Extraverted Sensing. How can it be spiritual?"

An Extraverted Sensing participant answered, "Remember earlier how I talked about peddling my bike along a country road, the sun warming my back, the breeze cooling my face, every motion speaking of being free in God's gift of creation? *That's* Extraverted Sensing."

The man stared for a moment, then said, "You mean we get to have fun?"

That's ES spirituality. They might sum it up, "Our Creator made an interesting world with endless possibilities for adventure and excitement, so let's enjoy it!" Keenly aware of the delights of the sights, sounds, smells, tastes, touches, and wonders of nature, whether in the majesty or in the details of their environment, their gratitude for all of it is the essence of their soulwork.

Many Extraverted Sensing types discover early on that they feel closest to God while physically out in nature, preferably with people whose company they enjoy—these pursuits are often their best spiritual paths.

> *The first time in my life I really felt spiritual was at a youth camp. We spent our days swimming, hiking, and challenging other cabins to Capture the Flag and counselor hunts. Each evening, we gathered around the campfire to sing and listen to a talk about God. Out there under the stars, with the chirps of crickets and the occasional cry of a loon, it seemed as if I could almost reach out and touch our Creator. As an adult, if my soul needs renewal, I try to go to "camp" again! I organize outings for my close friends—hiking, antiquing—once we even went to a dude ranch. Somewhere along the way we recreate the "campfire" experience as well, connecting with each other, with nature, and with God.*
>
> —Bryce, 43, school board official

Extraverted Sensing types often combine their soulwork with their daily activities, such as exercising, cleaning, lawn chores, or even commuting to work. Rather than compartmentalize their soulwork, they turn their thoughts over to the experiences they are having in the moment, celebrating them as they happen.

"Either one's belief system has practical value or it's pretty useless," Extraverted Sensing types might say. They tend to look for soulwork that will help them right now rather than the more complex or philosophical aspects of faith.

> *One of my friends, an all-star athlete, broke his neck in a freak accident. Thankfully he recovered full use of his limbs, but later he told me, "Lying there, facing the prospect of never walking again, I poured out my fears and doubts to our rabbi. He told me how God let Job and others be angry. I started to see that life would be okay, either way."*
>
> *This friend had faced what I feared most—losing my active lifestyle. At his advice, I worked out my own faith before I might desperately need it. From this great world, I can see there's a God; I know from my friend that God will be there in the tough times.*
>
> —Bern, 22, teacher

Occasionally, a sense of spiritual inadequacy can creep in because Extraverted Sensing types engage more sporadically in some of the spiritual disciplines that other types view as essential.

> *Once, I tried to tell a youth leader that I felt closest to God when I was outside, not in church. There, I could wonder about the magnitude of a being who could create the whole universe. Besides, sitting still, listening to lectures and set prayers didn't do much for me. The youth leader told me to get down on my knees and repent of my sins.*
> —Kate, 33, social worker

With such judgments falling on them, Extraverted Sensing types don't always find their way into organized religion; however, they may also see joining a spiritual community as the most pragmatic way to help others or to set aside some regular times to be with God.

Silent, structured, or solitary practices might strike them as the equivalent of "la-la land"—a waste of time that could be used for the active experiences that feed their souls.

Prayer

Rather than formal prayers or rituals, the Extraverted Sensing life of prayer often involves meditation in the moment, as an event, blessing, or need occurs. To them, praying at a set time each day or following a routine separates the spiritual from the rest of their lives. However, they find many ways to make prayer a regular, if not scheduled, part of their lives.

- They may join a small group of like-minded souls. These might be friends or people who are at the same stage of life as they are (who may quickly become friends). Often, praying or studying together is just part of the reason for gathering. At the same time, they might also head out for a bike ride, enjoy a delicious meal, or catch up on each other's lives before (or after) their time together.

> *Spirituality for me comes alive through relationships. I don't want to study, participate, or worship anonymously in large groups. I want to be with people who know about me and understand my joys and needs, and those of people closest to me.*
> —Jay, 52, consultant

- Extraverted Sensing types might also constantly look for new prayer experiences—visiting a more charismatic congregation a friend belongs to, walking a labyrinth, finding an outdoor service. They want to *try* these practices rather than read about them, and may continue to experiment and pick up additional helpful suggestions for soulwork from these experiences.

- Using their senses to call them to prayer is another technique. Extraverted Sensing types might place their favorite scented candle on the kitchen table as both a physical reminder to talk with God and, once lit, an added sensory experience for their prayer time. Gazing at a religious symbol such as the cross often focuses their thoughts. They might also post a picture of someone for whom they want to pray by their bedside or even on the refrigerator.

- They may want to wrap their prayer time into some other activity, focusing on the people in their lives as they walk, run, or bike, especially outside where the beauty of nature calls them to worship.

Worship

Extraverted Sensing types want worship to be as interesting as they make the rest of their lives, often bringing their gifts of spontaneity and fun to those whom they join in celebration. They prefer vibrant, joyful atmospheres where the senses can be engaged directly: uplifting music, appealing surroundings or activities to watch, or perhaps the aroma of incense or candles to ground their thoughts in past experiences. Less formal settings suit them best, especially when people dress casually and at least *appear* to enjoy the service or event.

- They seek services or rituals that change a bit from time to time. Too much predictability can cause them to stop paying attention, although they may feel guilty about their reaction if the form of worship is part of the tradition in which they were raised. They might wonder, "What's wrong with me that I can't appreciate what has worked for so many before me?"

My mom always said, "You don't have to be a Catholic like me, but someday you'll be glad you know God." Watching her worship and pray with sincerity all through my childhood convinced me that a

belief in God was important. Once out of her house, though, I visited other denominations and read about other religions. I found more meaning in campus ministry events than in formal church services. I need to keep adding new flavor to my spirituality or my zest for it fades away.
　　—Bram, 22, student

- True-life examples or visual aids help them focus on oral teachings.

  Often, sermons leave me looking out the windows, feeling as if sitting in the pews is a duty, not worship. But one minister makes things come alive. Once he brought in a tattered old leather suitcase and asked the kids to try to lift it during the children's sermon. They couldn't budge it. Then, during the adult sermon he pulled bricks out of it, labeled shame, guilt, jealousy, anger, pride—and talked about how these burdens we carry weigh us down and keep us from finding the joy God intended for us. Years later, when I start feeling one of those emotions, the thought of those bricks comes back to me.
  　　—Ted, 50, marketing executive

- Worship also comes about by celebrating, with thanks to the Creator, the milestones of life such as birthdays, anniversaries, or even the gift of a beautiful day.

If things are too staid, or if those around them seem to be passively listening rather than actively engaging, Extraverted Sensing types may leave to find a better fit for themselves. Or, they may take the role of a rebel—ignoring the formal codes, asking the tough questions, or avoiding all pretense or bureaucratic processes.

The group's conversation was so tiresome that I couldn't help but interject my reaction to a rather racy movie I'd seen the night before. The focus of my comment was the predictable and vapid story line that served only as a vehicle for luridness, but the others didn't get beyond the fact that I'd actually dared to see such trash. I rather enjoyed their shock. Not surprisingly, the group never invited me back!
　　—Maya, 58, dietician, married to a minister

Study

As for prayer and worship, Extraverted Sensing study often takes place with a group of friends. They look to apply what they are learning to real life and are less interested in theology than in how their faith can help them live more fully and also be of service to others.

- Rather than study for study's sake, they are more likely to take topical classes such as faith and parenting, workplace ethics, time management, or finances
- They enjoy hearing or reading about others' experiences. They might listen to inspiring speakers or find examples of how God works by reading biographies and novels as well as watching television or movies.
- Often, a desire for study comes about through a life event for which they need answers. Then, Extraverted Sensing types might read deeply, seek a class or seminar, or talk with those they view as wise.

My sister became involved in what we now know was a cult. To understand how she could accept the leader's distortions and rules, I read several books on cults—the practices, the psychology used, and news stories on several prominent cults. In my search, I figured out my own beliefs of right and wrong, but also learned that I was not comfortable in the role of judge—there are too many contradictory facts concerning many issues. When my sister emerged from the cult's influence and we reviewed her experiences together, I saw that my less complex view of issues was just right for me.
—Kayla, 36, teacher

Service

Most Extraverted Sensing types jump in with both feet when they see a real need. They are often aware of just what to do in a crisis and readily provide tangible help through running errands, providing transportation, filling sandbags as a river rises, or pruning trees for an elderly neighbor. For them, service is taking action to solve immediate problems concerning people, organizations, or the natural world.

- Extraverted Sensing types prefer working with other people in outcome-oriented teams, where they can *tangibly* see that their efforts make a difference. They enjoy single-focus projects where they can solve a problem or meet a need, then move on to another opportunity. They often know how to efficiently finish a task or provide appropriate resources.

- They might also volunteer for ongoing ministries that allow them to touch the lives of different people, such as visiting the sick and elderly, working with teens, or providing nursery care.

Several friends and I joined together to conduct recreational activities for teens. While we have a secular organization, we all are very aware of how God is at work in our lives and the lives of the teens. The spiritual questions these kids asked encouraged me to seek a more spiritual path for myself. So you might say I found myself and my spiritual roots by helping young people mature!
    —Perry, 32, factory supervisor

- Extraverted Sensing types also often have a knack for welcoming strangers, planning festivities, being positive, and gladly helping when asked. Because their lives in general are spontaneous, they are often grateful to friends who ask for their help.

I don't exactly fit the mold of eager volunteer, mainly because I'm never really sure of my schedule. But, a great friend runs a bunch of the maintenance activities at the synagogue. He only calls when he's working on something he knows I do well, like helping him build a boat for the children's play. Another friend always signs me up to flip pancakes for the youth breakfast, and then reminds me to show up. I truly appreciate that they know me well enough to know how I can help and that I want to if they help me by asking me!
    —Aaron, 26, retail store manager

Other Forms of Soulwork

With their love of life, Extraverted Sensing types find endless ways to tap into their spiritual side through activities, nature, being with others, or in tackling life's problems.

- They may seek to combine recreational activities with their soulwork by finding others with similar avocational interests (biking, fishing, sports teams, and so forth) and joined them on these types of outings. These relationships often lead to strong common bonds that make it possible to discuss spiritual matters.

I didn't join my church just to play softball, but when I heard there was a team, I knew I'd find some friends and people who look at life the way I do. Soon I was part of a Bible study after the games, too.
    —Tyrone, 29, pilot

- Extraverted Sensing types often create "retreats" from normal routines. Planned around fun activities, and by including close friends with whom meaningful discussion is possible, the outings often become spirit-filled.

My elderly mother, sister, and I spend the High Holy Days together. We visit arboretums, botanical gardens, or the small town where my grandparents grew up. These excursions allow us to share our family stories while experiencing our connections with our roots, the soil, and to earth and life itself.
    —Jason, 46, restaurant manager

- They also frequently focus their soulwork on finding help for problems they are facing. Often these experiences become tangible evidence that God is real and a part of our lives.

When I lost my job, a friend dragged me to a support group. I was surprised at how many mainstream business-executive types were there, sharing how essential spirituality was to their work. Their sincerity and integrity impressed me, but I was blown away by the amount of personal help they gave me as I searched for a new position. They didn't just sit around talking about how I might get help, they provided assistance themselves out of their convictions.
    —Leron, 34, business manager

In short, Extraverted Sensing spirituality helps all of us remember that
- life is a blessing;
- soulwork is part of life, not separate from it;
- what we do, not just what we think or say, matters;
- enjoying all the activities, sights, and wonders of life is reason enough to worship.

The Second Half of Life's Spiritual Journey

While Extraverted Sensing is about enjoying the present moment, eventually life grows short. Or, as do all personalities, the Extraverted Sensing types begin to wonder at midlife whether they have found sufficient meaning and purpose. If they continue on their current path, will they be ready for the future?

Often at this point, the Extraverted Sensing types have developed their natural spiritual path. Then, richness comes through their inferior function, Introverted Intuition. This involves

- developing a consistent, deliberate, intentional relationship with God;
- dialoguing internally and imaginatively about broad, enticing future possibilities;
- concentrating on what is unseen, inexplicable, and mystical about spirituality;
- looking at life's events with a sense of the reality of the impossible that involves purposes bigger than we can comprehend.

While Extraverted Sensing types may continue many of their favorite methods of soulwork, here are some examples of what they found as they journeyed on into Introverted Intuition:

At least once a year, I disengage from the real world and participate in a structured spiritual retreat. I take time to nurture my relationship with what is unseen in this world and contemplate the direction I'm headed. If I don't actually get away, my pragmatic side gets in the way of this. But when I do go, my goals and aspirations become crystal-clear guidance for the future—and the present!

I've started paying close attention to my dreams. When I was younger, I assumed they had no connection with real life. Now I find I can interpret them with ease and can rely on the information. I've also learned to write down my hunches. I don't always look for proof—now there are actually things I "just know."

Before, I only sensed God's presence when soaking up sunshine or marveling at the smooth movements of the horse I was riding. But now I'm comfortable living with an undefined Creator. Somehow I find new comfort in living with this "awesomeness" instead of viewing it as a disconcerting mystery. If I quiet my soul, I sometimes feel as if I am looking at what I might describe as "Glory" through a doorway.

I used to be concerned with God only to help me deal with the here and now. Those songs and teachings about eternal life held little appeal for me—what could be better than this world? Now, though, with the death of a close friend and my own recent illness, I've started exploring more about our souls after death, dreaming about what might be yet to come.

A friend gave me a framework that helps me tap into my sixth sense, highlighting the differences between our view and God's view of the world. There are a spiritual reality and a physical reality, an eternal perspective and a present perspective, the impact of our deeds and the deeds themselves, spiritual laws and physical laws, God-centered thinking and human-centered thinking, the unseen and the seen. We use this framework together to brainstorm the different perspectives a situation might present. It helps me look beyond the facts and my own experience, helping me find new understandings of the events of my life.

Any of the Introverted Intuition pathways (chapter 6) can bring this kind of rest and richness for Extraverted Sensing types if they allow their dominant functions a time of rest and let the Spirit guide their thoughts and actions.

ESTP

Extraversion Sensing
Thinking Perceiving

*Spirituality in the outer world of events
and adventure*

*Therefore everyone who hears these words of mine and puts them into
practice is like a wise man who built his house on the rock.*
—Matthew 7:24

Greatest Gifts

Making the most of the present moment; Seizing opportunities for
renewal for themselves and others, yet seeing reality and dealing with it
objectively and capably

Role in Community

Meeting practical needs in the most proficient way; Adding an energetic spark to any endeavor they find worthwhile; Reminding others of the
joys in this life

ESTPs tend to be action-oriented, outgoing, pragmatic, and resourceful. They like to be where the excitement is and where they can use their
quick thinking at just the right time to solve problems. They are to-the-
point, lively, and efficient. Enjoying life each day, they help others participate fully in the here and now.

Using their dominant function, Extraverted Sensing, is the natural
starting place for soulwork. However, their auxiliary or second function,
Introverted Thinking, calls them to pull back for introspection.

Soulwork through the Second Function

Through Introverted Thinking, ESTPs can choose among the options they see, define for themselves what is true and relevant, and bring their intellect to bear on their spiritual experiences.

Rather than total solitude for reflection, ESTPs might take part in regular classes or small groups that allow them to process topics or coursework in private, yet have the stimulus of group interactions.

Some ESTPs schedule time for meditation, organized study, or writing, especially if an early experience shows positive benefits to such practices.

Within these settings, ESTPs might seek to use Introverted Thinking by engaging in any of the exercises listed for that section (pages 145-149), with goals such as

- reordering priorities;
- reflecting on whether they are living by their principles;
- clarifying what matters most to them;
- setting goals and how they might be achieved;
- looking at costs and benefits or pros and cons of different choices.

All of these goals might help them bring clarity to their beliefs and depth to their soulwork.

> *I calmed down as I laid out some specific parameters for deciding how we might take care of my elderly mother. She disliked being alone. She needed to keep her cat. She had to be closer to my home. Narrowing the field like this gave me renewed energy to analyze the pros and cons of the remaining choices and brought about a useful solution to the dilemmas we faced.*
> —Gillian, 34, craftswoman

What Might Push ESTPs Away from Their Spiritual Path

With their drive for bringing their faith to bear on the rest of their lives and their emphasis on celebrating life as it unfolds, several factors can lead ESTPs to believe that their spiritual walk is not as important as other aspects of their lives. Common themes we heard from the people we interviewed included

- being drawn to the immediacies of life, not carving out time for the spiritual. ESTPs can easily fall into this trap since, in spiritual communities, it's hard to find the hands-on learning experiences they prefer and that help them apply their faith to real life.

- getting stuck by longing for tangible, direct proof of the unseen. If an experience doesn't provide dramatic, or at least recognizable, evidence of spirituality, ESTPs may feel the effort was useless or that they somehow missed the boat. They are especially vulnerable to this "trap" if those around them claim to have had profound experiences.
- failing to find like-minded souls, those who appreciate the lighter side of the spiritual journey. Since ESTPs often opt out of spiritual communities, finding others like themselves can be difficult.
- avoiding structure and schedule, especially if others are telling them the "right way" to pray or faulting them for missing regular worship. One of the greatest gifts people can give to an ESTP is the chance to explore and develop their own soulwork.

Trusted spiritual advisors, friends, and family can help ESTPs find an enriching spiritual path by
- talking openly about the difference faith has made in their lives, especially when facing struggles;
- joining with them for those adventures and activities that become spiritual in the moment;
- refraining from judgment as to what is and isn't spiritual;
- learning from ESTPs about the gift of each day as a reason to celebrate.

When Life Is Difficult

The fourth, or inferior, function for ESTPs is Introverted Intuition. With their emphasis on the present moment, tapping into the Introverted Intuitive realm of insights, hunches, and visions for the future is a struggle. In times of stress, the inferior function can erupt, changing ESTPs' behavior into a caricature of INFJs or INTJs for whom it is the dominant function.

For ESTPs in times of stress, the following circumstances might trigger the inferior function:
- When the present is no longer enjoyable, due to illness, physical disabilities, or damaged relationships, and they fear that things might not improve.
- When they can't control the time frames for making decisions about their future. They detest having their options cut off and try to wait for clear direction or sufficient information. Being

given too many future possibilities, with no clear direction, can heighten their frustration.

- When they can't take time to pursue the activities that bring them renewal.
- When the predicament imposes undue structure on their lives, as do chemotherapy schedules, the job search process, and many other situations.

Often, the worst times for ESTPs are when they bring all their energy and problem-solving skills to bear on a problem, then have reason to doubt they are working toward the right outcome. Perhaps they overused their dominant function, assuming things would continue in a straight pattern or failing to read any patterns under the surface of the events. Then everything about the future becomes doom and gloom, their inferior function Intuition taking a dark cast.

> *I'd kept my nose to the grindstone at work despite the massive layoffs and general atmosphere of doom and gloom. With ten years invested in a job that had basically been satisfying, I was in no hurry to find anything new. Then one day I realized that I was like the little Dutch boy whose one finger in the dike held back the floodwaters—but no one was going to come to my aid. Only when the evidence became overwhelming did it occur to me that I needed to turn my energy toward finding a new job.*
> —Wali, 44, sales

In these situations, ESTPs might be uncharacteristically miserable, tired, or hypersensitive. They might also avoid the activities that usually feed their bodies and spirits, instead withdrawing, locked up in their dire predictions of the future. When these symptoms appear, a totally different approach to soulwork often helps. ESTPs might purposefully pursue Introverted Intuition. Its conscious use requires the ESTP to shut down what is usually easiest—Extraverted Sensing—which may have gotten out of control. By doing so, ESTPs can slow down to concentrate and focus, getting in touch with their own dreams and possibilities for the future.

Ways to consciously engage the Intuitive function include:

- Develop contingency plans. Consider the impact of a decision six or twelve months from now, or even two to five years into the future. If the worst really does happen, what are the options?

Mapping out available help or possible different courses can lessen despair over losses.

- Watch future-oriented television programs or read books that involve theories or hypotheses about what could be. Topics might include scientific developments or even science fiction, substituting an imaginary journey for ESTPs' normal, pragmatic approach.
- Engage in activities that require thinking through possible outcomes. One ESTP played tabletop world conquest games where he had to consider several different strategies. Others envisioned remodeling projects, daydreamed about finding a financial windfall, or imagined a successful personal, family, or business adventure.

In the chosen activity, the key is backing away from uncontrolled negative thinking and engaging in a process that makes the future again look worth striving toward. As one ESTP put it, "Once I write down the worst thing that can happen, and then come up with a way I'd deal with it, I can get on with the moment."

As an ESTP, I am thankful for
my love of this life,
my realistic grasp of situations,
my resourcefulness and quick responsiveness,
the way I can catch the joys of the moment.

When life is difficult, I can find support by
making time to pause and reflect,
envisioning the future with positive expectations,
assessing my true priorities.

To honor myself and my pathway to God, I can
search for ways to integrate soulwork and the activities I enjoy,
seek the company of others who find spirituality in the midst of life,
retreat, if only rarely, to give my spiritual side the attention it needs.

ESFP

Extraversion Sensing
Feeling Perceiving

Spirituality in the outer world of events and people

A cheerful heart is good medicine.
—Proverbs 17:22

Greatest Gifts

Lighting up any setting with their easygoing nature, enthusiasm, and love of life; Accepting people and situations as they are in a straightforward yet sensitive way

Role in Community

Serving as a resource of time and talents; Reminding others how to appreciate God through the five senses; Adding warmth and informality to spiritual endeavors through their desire to put others at ease

---

ESFPs tend to be fun-loving, friendly, outgoing, and exuberant. They are relationship-oriented and in touch with people's needs for encouragement, comfort, and inclusion. They are sympathetic and generous with their time and support. ESFPs engage others in living life to its fullest. Practical and realistic, they are often where the action is.

Using their dominant function, Extraverted Sensing, is the natural starting place for soulwork. However, their auxiliary or second function, Introverted Feeling, calls them to pull back for reflection.

Soulwork through the Second Function

Introverted Feeling allows ESFPs to redefine what is important to them, explore how their values might influence different courses of action, and understand their own reactions to situations, ideas, or the actions of others.

Rather than seeking total solitude for reflection, ESFPs often head out for long walks with a close, understanding companion. Or, a quiet, natural setting might let them tap into their Introverted Feeling processes.

> *My friend joined me for walks frequently during the month following my mother's protracted illness and eventual death. I realized that I felt guilty about my sense of relief at not having to nurse her anymore. My friend helped me see that after my day-in, day-out care of her, my relief from the heavy physical and emotional burden was natural, not selfish.*
>
> —Joan, 29, recreation leader

ESFPs might arrange to be home alone for a few hours to gain reflection time, escape to favorite natural surroundings, or take part in a guided reflection session to use Introverted Feeling. Any of the exercises listed in the Feeling section (pages 193-198) might also help them with goals such as

- clarifying their values;
- understanding their own emotional reactions to a situation;
- thinking through the impact of options on each of the people involved;
- setting boundaries as to what they will and won't do to help someone;
- identifying any areas where they are not living out their values.

All of these areas, the gifts of Introverted Feeling, might help them bring clarity to their beliefs and depth to their soulwork.

> *When life is rosy, I seldom just sit by the lake—I swim, boat, ski, fish, or sail. However, when the future seems dark and heavy, I take a blanket down by the shore and gaze at the waves lapping the beach, the families of ducks paddling by, the clouds reflected on the water. I observe the cycles of the seasons and gain hope that the seasons of my life will pass on to warmth and spring again.*
>
> —Jessie, 30, secretary

What Might Push ESFPs Away from Their Spiritual Path

With their interest in bringing their faith to bear on the rest of their lives and their emphasis on celebrating life as it unfolds, several factors can lead ESFPs to believe that their spiritual walk is not as important as other aspects of their lives. Common experiences we heard from the ESFPs we interviewed included the following:

- When their spiritual communities or influential people around them require that spirituality be done formally or "by the book."
- When ESFPs allow the needs of friends, the weather, or choices of activity to have more pull than any of their spiritual pursuits.
- Becoming too busy, too involved, and overloaded in helping others. ESFPs can overlook their own spiritual needs to the point that their helping becomes an excuse or justification for putting off their soulwork.
- Engaging in any activity, hobby, or spiritual path so intensely that they eventually lose the joy it used to bring.

Trusted spiritual advisors, friends, and family can help ESFPs find an enriching spiritual path by

- talking with them about what God might be doing beyond what is experienced in the here and now;
- helping them question what is best for them in a given circumstance, yet letting them choose their own course of action;
- gently guiding them toward spiritual events or practices that suit their path that they haven't yet explored;
- taking time to listen and talk with them one-on-one.

When Life Is Difficult

The fourth, or inferior, function for ESFPs is Introverted Intuition. With ESFPs' emphasis on the present moment, tapping into the Introverted Intuitive realm of insights, hunches, and visions for the future can be a struggle. In times of stress, the inferior function can erupt, changing ESFPs' behavior into a caricature of INTJs and INFJs for whom Introverted Intuition is the dominant function.

For ESFPs in times of stress, the following circumstances might trigger the inferior function:

- When circumstances force too much speculation, creative problem-solving, or long-range planning, so that too much time is spent using their inferior function. ESFPs then often get caught up in negative thinking about the future, adding to their gloom.

- When the situation causes them to acknowledge the march of time and the finality of separation. ESFPs become vulnerable to stress when relationships are permanently severed.
- When the present is no longer enjoyable and they are uncertain of whether the future will be better. ESFPs can be particularly depressed by the diminishment of their own physical health or capabilities through injury, illness, or aging.
- When they are forced to add too much structure to their lives, be it in pursuit of helping others or meeting their own needs.

Often, the worst times for ESFPs are when they concentrate so hard on meeting the immediate needs of other people in a situation that they neglect themselves. Perhaps they overused their dominant function, continuing in a flurry of activity rather than face the forebodings they feel. Then everything about the future becomes doom and gloom, their inferior function Intuition taking a dark cast.

> *When my husband's best friend was diagnosed with terminal cancer, we did everything we could for his family. We looked after the children so that he and his wife could have some time alone. I organized meal delivery and made all the arrangements for special equipment so that he could be nursed at home. I helped plan a prayer service and checked that it met his spiritual preferences. I made sure that my husband encouraged our other mutual friends to support him. When our friend finally died, I realized that I'd taken no opportunity to come to grips with what this dear friend's life meant to me. I couldn't even attend the funeral. I needed to withdraw from all of my activities for several days as I grieved.*
> —Nancy, 48, homemaker

In these situations, ESFPs might vent negative thoughts about the future, or make decisions, even major ones, that have little to do with their normal priorities. When these symptoms appear, a totally different approach to soulwork often helps. ESFPs might purposefully pursue Introverted Intuition. Its conscious use requires ESFPs to shut down what is usually easiest—Extraverted Sensing—which may have gotten under control. In doing so, ESFPs will slow down to concentrate and focus, getting in touch with their own dreams and possibilities for the future.

Ways to consciously engage the Intuitive function include

- becoming deeply involved with a creative interest that might open up the imagination to new avenues for soulwork. ESFPs might consider themes of wholeness or spirituality while painting, writing, and listening to or performing music.
- designing or planning a complex future event like retirement or financing children's education.
- spending time in solitude, reading for enjoyment, or reflecting and journaling on the events and concerns of life. ESFPs can look beyond the facts for different interpretations and implications for the future.

In the chosen activity, the key is allowing their thoughts and imagination to again ponder a future that aligns with their values and drive to enjoy life as it comes—and to help others do the same. One ESFP described, "Now I can better use my imagination to understand the present and the future. For example, when I was laid off recently, I considered what my future might have been there. In truth, other places and vistas will hold far greater meaning and purpose than the job I was once afraid of losing!"

As an ESFP, I am thankful for
> my enjoyment of each new day and the fresh wonders it brings,
> the varied ways I offer practical help to others,
> the enthusiasm I add to each endeavor and to those around me,
> my openness to exploring, experimenting, and experiencing spirituality in different ways.

When life is difficult, I can find support by
> seeking support from those who know me well,
> reserving some time so that I will have renewed energy for myself as well as for others,
> focusing on the unseen, those inexplicable aspects of our lives.

To honor myself and my pathway to God, I can
> see God in the here and now by experiencing the Creator in all of creation,
> connect with others to join in celebrating our spiritual journeys,
> become comfortable with listening to my dreams and hopes for the future.

CHAPTER FOUR

INTROVERTED SENSING:

The Time-Honored
Spiritual Path

Introverted Sensing Spirituality
ISTJ, ISFJ

Using experiences, the examples of others, and time-tested traditions to develop patterns of soulwork that help in day-to-day living.

"**M**y favorite statement of faith," an Introverted Sensing type told us, "was an advertisement for a monastery that proclaimed

We Haven't Changed in 2,000 Years.

I *am* open to new practices," he continued, "but first and foremost I'm intrigued by practices that have stood the test of time."

Introverted Sensing spirituality is organized and practical but never boring. They are realists, clearly aware of good and evil, the practical and impractical, and the useful and useless activities all around them. These opposing ways of the world lead them to search for concrete answers to major issues of spirituality. Their goal is a spiritual awareness that allows them to use their faith for guidance for day-to-day living.

> *My spirituality became concrete as I studied the Amish, hoping to understand how they integrate religion, family life, and work. More than any other group of Christians, they seem to "walk the talk." Their system seems successful—little alcoholism, addiction, abuse, crime— and about seventy-five percent of the children choose to remain in the community. Strange, since they are generally thought of as "backward," not modern. They focus on group values, not themselves, and they view work as a blessing, not "Adam's curse." As I work with other people, I constantly urge them to think in terms of what would be best for everyone, not their own needs.*
> —Ford, 58, executive coach

What they see and experience helps Introverted Sensing types evaluate and understand their private beliefs. Spiritual understandings often come from real situations involving real people. Lessons from the lives of those they admire or direct experiences with the observable wonders of life—such as the birth of a child—often draw them along in their spiritual journey. They begin to sense "something" besides themselves at work in daily events that defy explanation, unexpected or unearned acts of kindness, or the brightening of people's moods.

> *My spirituality means that I do those things that serve the common good. I keep my soul open to God's presence through prayer, meditation, walking in natural settings, participating in my spiritual community, and doing things that directly help others.*
> —Jon, 23, child-care provider

One stated, "Faith is a process of growing both in understanding and in dependence. Little by little, I've found enough concrete proof that I can trust God with the details of my life." Soulwork that makes their faith more tangible and oriented to what needs doing at the present time is most appealing to Introverted Sensing types. They want to understand how their traditions apply to specific situations, how to behave responsibly, and follow through on what they believe God wants them to do.

Many Introverted Sensing types, with their desire for clear structure and order, appreciate the richness of traditions surrounding creeds, religious rituals, and holy days. While they may accept many aspects of the faith in which they were raised, rather than it being a blind following, their acceptance comes from an acknowledgment of the considerable merit of ceremonies, principles, and values that have worked for generations. Their faith is far from unexamined. In any spiritual pursuit, Introverted Sensing types want to grasp its purpose and benefits, through logic or through its impact on people.

> *I've always been grateful to my parents for the early religious exposure they gave me. I never viewed the services and ceremonies as rote, but simply the right thing to do. I knew that my mother, grandfather, great-grandfather, and maybe even generations further back had done the same things and held the same beliefs, giving God a major place in their lives.*
>
> *To me, providing spiritual training is as much a part of parenting as feeding or educating children. Those who don't are robbing their kids. Whether the children accept everything or not, a faith tradition gives them a history lesson, moral instruction, and values.*
> —Eden, 39, homemaker

Introverted Sensing types are concerned about seriously carrying out their faith's directives in the real world. Some choose to lead while others prefer to remain supportive, in the background.

Prayer

Prayer for Introverted Sensing types is often organized or based on traditions. They internalize the methods they have been taught and use them well, but they may also read books or take classes to learn about new, effective ways to pray.

- Introverted Sensing types might search for a comfortable or effective method of prayer, through study or reading, preferring a precise program to random or unstructured prayer times. While not all have schedules that allow for it, many Introverted Sensing types prefer to have a set time for prayer and a set place as well. They may enrich this time by writing in a special journal, sipping a fragrant tea, or sitting in a favorite rocker or chair. They often also use a daily devotional guide, such as a booklet with a meditation for each day of the month.

- They are often drawn to praying systematically for others, keeping track of prayer requests in journals or in other ways.

My friends often ask me to pray for them. They comment that I remember the concerns each person raises and add an appreciation for the constant role our Creator plays. Really, it's the sort of detail-oriented solo work I enjoy the most. Others might provide advice or a casserole, but I usually pray with or for someone in crisis.
—Amanda, 31, medical technician

- Meeting regularly with a small group for prayer and study typically gives Introverted Sensing types a regular, disciplined approach for their spirituality. While they often cultivate supportive and close relationships within these groups, they also like to keep prayer as the group's focus if that is their primary purpose for gathering.
- Memories and traditions play an important role in prayer and meditation, especially when they have been carefully weighed and found to be of value.

Our family life revolved around the traditions, celebrations, stipulations, and activities of Judaism. I never questioned my faith, it was so much a part of what we did as a family. In those early years, the Law provided both a structure and a haven for me. It wasn't until college, when I took formal classes about my faith, that I had questions. I struggled with the legalistic positions on the role of evil—when bad things happen to good people. Eventually I understood that questions and beliefs can go hand in hand. I remind myself that I'm not God and I don't have to grasp the whole picture to be faithful.
—Margo, 52, librarian

Worship

Introverted Sensing types often prefer a rhythm of predictability to worship—not because they dislike variety, but because the rituals tap into the history and grandeur of their faith.

- Often, traditional liturgical practices provide a sense of rightness and completeness to their worship. Some Introverted Sensing types describe how the regular rituals provide weekly renewal, a sense of going back to their roots. They appreciate knowing in advance if a service will be altered from the format they generally follow.
- Since they themselves tend to be quiet and orderly, Introverted Sensing types often like their worship to be the same way.
- They often enjoy hearing about the "heroes" of faith—how God worked through these heroes or how their faith changed their lives.

Study

Introverted Sensing types are often lifelong learners, constantly looking to increase their understanding of God and improve their ability to put that knowledge to use in their lives.

- Introverted Sensing types usually prefer study groups with clear goals or defined materials. They may look to recommended reading lists, perhaps from clergy, religious magazines, or other knowledgeable sources. While they trust their own judgment, they often feel that looking to the wisdom of others will help them use their study time most effectively. For example, they might read a book with study questions at the end of each chapter or attend a structured study of sacred texts.

    While my small group uses all sorts of materials, I must admit I prefer the fill-in-the-blank Bible studies—read a chapter, answer the questions, apply the concepts to my life. I know how long it will take me each week, I know when I'm done. I'm not trying to limit my effort, but rather, that sense of accomplishment makes me feel that I'm on track spiritually.
    —Gayle, 45, computer analyst

- Introverted Sensing types might also seek long-term study programs: a series of classes on spiritual growth, a program that provides certification for a volunteer experience they hope to participate in, or even a degree program, especially if they weren't able to pursue formal studies at an early age. Through these efforts, they often strive to understand how the teachings and practices of their traditions can be useful for modern day-to-day living.

Even the words "Systematic Theology" appeal to me. I know the subject will be presented objectively, the concepts will build on each other logically, and the topic of theology holds my interest. For me, doctrinal statements are worthy of study and the creeds that connect me with generations of long ago are essential. Either these basic elements are solid and can hold water, or I'll pursue my spiritual life elsewhere.
    —Ted, 48, employee training manager

- They may also study tangible examples of faith in action. They may learn more about compassion from watching someone empathize with people experiencing loss than through classroom work on counseling.

Service

Service and spirituality are indivisible for many Introverted Sensing types. Their soulwork helps them understand their purpose in life and what they can do for others.

- They may actively serve others one-to-one or by supporting efforts in which they believe.

    I think people like me are wired to carry the "burden" of identifying with the suffering of others and the world. By nature, I feel compelled to do something about it.
    —Barbara, 60, nurse

- Some Introverted Sensing types serve as a resource to others struggling to handle matters of faith. Because they can easily recall facts and details that assist in making decisions, they can often discern inequities or the heart of a matter and provide useful solutions.
- Usually, their spirituality is evident in their dedication to any endeavor they undertake. "Either our faith makes a tangible difference in how we live or, perhaps, we have no faith," they might say. They look for settings where others share their values for responsibility, loyalty, and steadfastness in faith.

My soulwork is part of my life. In my job as director of community services for the elderly, I ensure that the meals delivered each day meet the individual health requirements of each recipient. I feel that on a

daily basis I provide the hand of God tangibly to those in need—a
common theme in all faith traditions.
    —Heather, 57, social services director

Other Forms of Soulwork

With their tireless pursuit of practical and effective soulwork, Introverted
Sensing types find endless ways to tap into their spiritual side through day-
to-day activities as well as by joining in organized events.

- They may concentrate on looking for evidence of God in the
  details of life. Often they seek time alone to reflect on their lives,
  discerning what God has been doing.

  After my husband died, I was struck by the many small ways in which
  I'd been prepared for my new life as a widow. Ed had been unable
  to go with me to church for some time, so I was used to being alone
  there. Our home repairs were all completed, so I had no maintenance
  worries. With his dietary problems, I'd grown accustomed to cooking
  for one. As much as I miss him, I have these small reminders that God
  has been with me all along.
      —Marjorie, 75, retired teacher

- They may participate in retreats for renewal, especially in quiet,
  peaceful or beautiful settings that allow for relaxation and introspection.
- Another activity that feeds their souls is completing hands-on projects or crafts that meet practical needs and allow for self-expres-
  sion. With their ability to attend to details, Introverted Sensing
  types can express their soulwork through meticulous activities
  such as quilting, woodworking, or handling all the specifics of a
  project.

In short, Introverted Sensing spirituality helps all of us remember that
- traditions and history bring richness to soulwork,
- our faith should be evident in our lives,
- reflecting on what God is doing can increase our sense of God's
  presence today, in the here and now,
- setting aside time for study and prayer establishes a rhythm for
  living.

The Second Half of Life's Spiritual Journey

While Introverted Sensing is about understanding the role of spirituality in our day-to-day lives, all too often life's struggles demand that we deal with things we can't predict. Or, as do all personalities, the Introverted Sensing types begin to wonder whether they have found sufficient meaning and purpose. If they continue on their current path, will they be ready for the future?

Often at this stage, the Introverted Sensing types have developed their natural spiritual path. Then, richness comes through their inferior function, Extraverted Intuition. This involves

- experiencing the sacred in future possibilities and exploring idealism in self, others, and different opportunities;
- being attracted to new avenues and untried practices for spiritual expression;
- exploring with others the mysteries of spirituality and accepting things that have neither concrete proof nor practical applications;
- using imagination to discern new insights or muse about the big meanings behind simple stories and commonplace events.

While they may continue many of their favorite methods of soulwork, here are some examples of what they found as they journeyed on into Extraverted Intuition.

Now that I have the time, I decided to take a creative writing class. It's a very spontaneous process. We take a topic such as "God's love" and just write our thoughts about it. I'm often amazed at the insights I come up with when I practice making associations and connections.

All my life I've viewed everything as a project to organize. More recently, I've tried to relinquish that "project manager" approach to my spiritual life. I let friends choose the books we'll study and the practices we'll try. I'm exploring new music as a way to open my mind to other ways of thinking of God. I even joined friends at a retreat center without checking out the scheduled activities for the weekend. I went with the flow!

A few years ago, I sensed that my spiritual routine had gone dry. I needed some unpredictability. I visited different places of worship, of my own faith and some different religions. A little hand-clapping, different songs, more emotion, strikingly fresh prayers . . . mine was a sort of bread-and-butter spirituality—good, stable, and wholesome but a bit stale. Every now and then a bit of "new wine" freshens my soul!

Before, I enjoyed classes that used day-to-day examples and emphasized practical applications. Now, I'm drawn more and more to global themes and subject matter. Because my own small corner of life is pretty well organized, my curiosity draws me to new knowledge in other arenas.

These days as I walk my dog in the evenings, I often ponder the magnitude of God's creation. I let the images float by and use them as a way to reminisce about the beauty of the world. My inner sense for having to have my every act be useful has toned down somewhat. My "flights of fancy" offer new vistas!

Any of the Extraverted Intuition pathways (chapter 5) can bring this kind of rest and richness if Introverted Sensing types allow their dominant functions a time of rest and let the Spirit guide their thoughts and actions.

ISTJ

Introversion Sensing Thinking Judging

Spirituality in the inner world of experiences and organizing principles

Hold them in the highest regard in love because of their work.
—1 Thessalonians 5:13

Greatest Gifts

Seeing what is; Using their internal awareness of what has worked in the past; Conscientiously and dutifully bringing order and logic to all they do

Role in Community

Upholding and conserving the splendor of tradition; Building clear structures; Modeling responsibility and follow-through; Using past experience to provide stability to the present

---

ISTJs tend to be systematic, painstaking, thorough, and hardworking. They honor their commitments, keep track of specifics, follow standard operating procedures (when they make sense), and get their work done on time. Careful with details, clear about facts, they are dependable, straightforward, and stable.

Using their dominant function, Introverted Sensing, is the natural starting place for soulwork. However, their auxiliary or second function, *Extraverted Thinking,* calls them to determine how to live out their principles and faith in the real world.

Soulwork through the Second Function

Extraverted Thinking calls the ISTJ to find some sort of spiritual community. They might seek a small group with a trusting setting for deep conversation, or they might seek a large community with ample opportunities to act on what they believe.

ISTJs understand that their own experiences need to be analyzed through their logical principles for them to be most effective. Further, the experiences of others can broaden their point of reference as they work to establish those standards. Meeting with people to discuss and debate the truth about issues of faith provides a sound basis to guide their actions.

> As an introverted male, sharing my problems with anyone, let alone another man, is extremely difficult. Recently though, I joined a men's fellowship group. Through our questioning and critiquing of each other's core principles, I've been able to build a framework for my spirituality. In addition, we've developed a level of trust with each other that allows us to talk about personal struggles.
> —Anders, 37, administrator

Within these settings, ISTJs might seek to use Extraverted Thinking by engaging in any of the exercises listed for Thinking (pages 145-149) with goals such as

- gathering different viewpoints;
- working with others to determine what is and isn't true;
- evaluating the merits of different interpretations, beliefs, or practices;
- working out their own personal standards;
- joining with people to act on their principles in tangible ways.

All of these might help them bring clarity to their beliefs and breadth to their soulwork.

> I used to struggle with questions like, "If God is sovereign and already knows what I want, why should I bother praying?" Through studying with others, I now understand that prayer affects how I might handle a situation or approach a change. Through it I can be a part of the answer—prayer has become a more rational process for me.
> —Tad, 54, engineer

What Might Push ISTJs Away from Their Spiritual Path

While many ISTJs continue to find richness in the traditions they were raised in, several factors can lead them to believe that faith has no relevance for the work of real life. Common themes we heard from the people we interviewed included

- finding that the behavior of "spiritual" people does not always match their speech. Even though it's only common sense to expect that some people are not all they say they are, ISTJs still can be turned off by the hypocrisy of people (especially spiritual leaders) or institutions.

  While I have fond childhood memories of choir, youth groups, roast beef dinners, and camps, I have not been successful in providing that same experience for my children. I think this is primarily because as an adult I see "faithful" people gossiping about each other and generally acting on their spiritual values only *when they're in a spiritual setting.*
  —Andrea, 48, computer programmer

- having too many responsibilities to add the "burden" of spirituality. Many ISTJs are already involved in giving, serving others through roles at work, in the community, or with their family. However, when ISTJs pursue a spiritual path that doesn't require attendance or involvement in an organized spiritual community, they can feel guilty that they don't make room for it in their busy lives.

- being in environments that place little emphasis on soulwork. Especially affected are ISTJs whose families of origin ridiculed or abandoned religion. Without any direct experiences to influence their opinions, ISTJs may not be open to new ideas related to the spiritual realm.

- setting standards for their spirituality that are too high. ISTJs can be all too aware of their own needs for improvement. Coupled with their focus on doing good deeds and solving practical problems, ISTJs may find their spiritual efforts come up short of their expectations.

  As willing as I am to help, I need to know from others that my efforts are useful. Otherwise, I sense I'm not doing what I thought I could and then find myself demoralized.
  —Beverly, 42, small-business owner

Trusted spiritual advisors, friends, and family can help ISTJs find an enriching spiritual path by

- offering specific, real-life examples of soulwork, especially ones with practical applications;
- appreciating the necessity for details when bringing plans to fruition and offering assistance to share their burden;
- providing ways to relax and laugh, keeping the focus on the big picture and the overall meaning of faith;
- supporting their ideas or decisions, upholding them with their actions and prayers.

When Life Is Difficult

The fourth, or inferior, function for ISTJs is Extraverted Intuition. With their emphasis on the present moment, tapping into the Introverted Intuitive realm of insights, hunches, and visions for the future can be a struggle. In times of stress, the inferior function can erupt, changing ISTJs' behavior into a caricature of ENFPs and ENTPs for whom Extraverted Intuition is the dominant function.

For ISTJs in times of stress, the following circumstances might trigger the inferior function:

- When the situation forces them to depart too far from their normal routine or familiar tasks—that is, what ISTJs know will work.
- When people offer nonspecific advice or help. ISTJs keep their commitments. When ISTJs offer to help, they will follow through with tangible assistance, so they are disappointed when others do not do the same.

  As we awaited the arrival of our new baby who we knew had major health problems, I grew frustrated with all of the platitudes even our closest friends offered. Don't say, "I'd love to lend a hand"—say you'll mow the lawn, drive my kids to soccer practice, or stay at home with our other children. And don't say everything will be soon be normal again, because it may not be. We will have to redefine what is normal after this blows over.
  —Barrett, 29, attorney

- When they are asked to create something entirely new in response to changing circumstances, especially if little clear direction is given.

- When they look toward the future and all options and possibilities seem bleak.

Dental school had been my goal for nearly six years; yet there I was, just five months into the program, when I realized that I had no aptitude for the sculpture work that makes up the majority of a dentist's day. The thought of completing the program, knowing I'd struggle with the skills, was paralyzing. I felt that I had no choice but to drop out of school and try some different work before investing any further in education. Fortunately, a friend helped me rethink the facts—I was very close to a degree in chemistry and with little effort I could at least graduate and get a job.
—Tara, 36, chemical engineer

Often, the worst times for ISTJs are when they continue on the same track of reliability and efficiency, as if sheer effort will prevail. If things don't improve, they start to question their abilities or even whether their sense of duty was misplaced. They may further isolate themselves by working harder, but probably not smarter, until fatigue or illness sets in.

We experienced a significant family crisis several years ago. The distress was so severe that I lost twenty-five pounds, became an insomniac, and grew despondent. During that time I did not miss one day of work. Only a small handful of close, personal friends knew of my difficulties. All of my pain was dealt with privately. On the surface, things often appeared status quo to others. I finally took some time off and sought professional counseling, even though it was very hard for me to do both.
—Rosalie, 51, bookkeeper

In these situations, ISTJs may have trouble handling details and specifics, usually their strengths. They may become overly impulsive. Or, they may worry obsessively about the future. When these symptoms appear, a totally different approach to soulwork often helps. ISTJs might *purposefully* pursue Extraverted Intuition. Its *conscious use* requires that the ISTJ shut down what is usually easiest—Introverted Sensing—which may have gotten out of control. By doing so, the ISTJ can open up to new ideas, possibilities, information, and solutions.

Ways to consciously engage the Intuitive function include:
- Imagining the worst possible outcome, then planning the best approach. Often this process surfaces a better awareness of what

is involved. Then ISTJs can use a step-by-step approach to work toward resolution.

- Concentrating on the big picture—determine what will *really* matter a year or five years from now. What is the overall goal, not the specific details? What could possibly change and what effects will that have?
- Joining with others to create something from scratch that's engaging and entertaining. For example, ISTJs might join a theater group, take a cruise, or go to another locale to gain a fresh perspective.

In the chosen activity, the key is to break away from both routine and uncontrolled negative thinking by engaging in a process that opens up alternatives. "I need to think past the mistakes I may have made and how they might lead to catastrophe," sums up an ISTJ. "Then I can find a new avenue to plan and follow."

As an ISTJ, I am thankful for
my gifts of sensibility and logic,
my awareness of the merit of learning from and building on past experiences,
my ability to follow through on commitments,
the ease with which I handle details and facts.

When life is difficult, I can find support by
looking for guidance from what has worked before and how things are resolved through faith,
turning over some of my responsibilities to others,
asking for help to assess the big picture—the larger meaning.

To honor myself and my pathway to God, I can
seek the practices that fit into my routine,
understand and apply unchanging truths in this changing world,
explore other traditions or spiritual disciplines to open the boundaries of my soul without violating what I know to be true.

ISFJ

Introversion Sensing Feeling Judging

Spirituality in the inner world of experience and unifying values

Pursue righteousness, godliness, faith, love, endurance, gentleness.
—*1 Timothy 6:1, NRSV*

Greatest Gifts

Approaching reality in a sensitive, helpful, orderly, and matter-of-fact way; Understanding what circumstances realistically mean for themselves and others

Role in Community

Offering tangible and dignified service that meets the needs of specific individuals while honoring order and tradition; Enrolling others to contribute cooperatively to the spiritual community

ISFJs tend to be dependable, considerate, and conscientious. They value harmonious settings with well-defined roles and responsibilities and practical ways to be useful. Each person's welfare is important to them. They dutifully conserve resources while organizing things to meet the needs of people they serve.

Using their dominant function, Introverted Sensing, is the natural starting place for soulwork. However, their auxiliary or second function, *Extraverted Feeling,* fosters a need for gathering with others, whether in a small group or large community.

Soulwork through the Second Function

Viewing their community as a place of service, ISFJs act out their devotion and loyalty, often as islands of calm to those around them. Community also allows ISFJs to apply their devotion and organizational skills to the common good.

ISFJs often seek people who share similar preferences for learning and fellowship experiences. When people share similar beliefs as well, the ISFJ feels comfortable that enrichment, not contention, will result.

> *Meeting regularly with others helps me reinforce my already-strong spirituality. I enjoy the encouragement and spirit of support and nourishment that comes from others who also value the same spiritual traditions and want to keep the historical aspects of our faith alive. My skills and talents are needed as well—as long as I can organize our meetings, I'll feel a vital part of the group.*
>
> —Anne, 71, retired records technician

The Feeling function also helps ISFJs evaluate which of their activities merit their time and attention. Because they see what needs doing and do it often before others even become aware, they need to care for themselves and allow others to do likewise.

> *When my wife was very ill, some of our close friends were so helpful. The men took me out for lunch while the women stayed at our home. I knew that my wife's needs were being met and I had a chance to be with friends who listened, laughed, and shared their own fears about losing a spouse. By interacting with them, I gained new perspectives on my situation.*
>
> —Roy, 66, retired religious professional

Within these settings, ISFJs might seek to use their second function, Extraverted Feeling, by engaging in any of the exercises listed for the Extraverted Feeling section (pages 193-197) with spiritual goals such as

- talking through their own feelings and impressions,
- looking for examples of God at work in the lives of others,
- finding role models for their spiritual journey,
- reaching out to others in caring service,
- forming deep relationships for their intellectual, social, and spiritual endeavors.

All of these might help them bring clarity to their beliefs and breadth to their soulwork.

What Might Push ISFJs Away from Their Spiritual Path

With their affinity for tradition, order, and kindness, life can bring experiences to ISFJs that lead them to doubt the wisdom of a spiritual path. Common themes we heard from the people we interviewed included

- experiencing circumstances that lack love, courtesy, or harmony. Many ISFJs find it difficult to entertain thoughts of a compassionate Creator when their life circumstances are devoid of the premises of doing good and following the rules.

> *My mother's belief was full of judgments and "thou shalt nots" and I could not accept this. I had to find my own belief system. Because I did not feel loved as a child, I did not think of God as a loving, caring being. Only when I had the experience of being fully accepted by others close to me was I able to grasp that God was loving.*
>
> —Marissa, 45, team-building consultant

- knowing that not everyone's contributions are honored, even their own. Because much of their devoted efforts take place behind the scenes, ISFJs can feel forgotten. Their input may not be acknowledged even when it is vital to the task or to others. ISFJs might begin to feel that either they or their ideas aren't important and therefore quietly withdraw from those settings.
- finding that spiritual organizations, their leaders, or their members lack integrity. If someone, especially in a leadership position, does not model what they preach, or a trusted structure or tradition stumbles, ISFJs may leave it rather than put up with the discrepancy between words and action.
- feeling that they failed in spite of doing everything the best that they could. ISFJs can have intense feelings of guilt or shame and thus withdraw from God when something bad happens to a child, a relationship, or a cause they cared about.

> *As a mother, I did the best I could and yet my oldest child committed suicide. I prayed so intensely for my son's depression to lift, and it did for awhile, but then it came back with the deadliest result.*

My soul seems unable to move beyond this tragedy, yet I long for it to do so.
    —Pamela, 56, executive secretary

Trusted spiritual advisors, friends, and family can help an ISFJ find an enriching spiritual path by

- serving as a model, encourager, and connection to rich experiences;
- offering to relieve some of the ISFJ's responsibilities since he or she often finds it hard to ask for assistance;
- taking time to study and discuss spiritual issues that are of concern, especially if the ISFJ is overwhelmed by feelings of inadequacy or failure;
- showing that they care through actions, not just words.

When Life Is Difficult

The fourth, or *inferior,* function for ISFJs is Extraverted Intuition. With the ISFJ's emphasis on the present moment, tapping into the Extraverted Intuitive spiritual realm of insights, hunches, and visions for the future can be a struggle.

In times of stress, the inferior function can erupt, changing the ISFJ's behavior into a caricature of ENTPs and ENFPs for whom it is the *dominant* function. For ISFJs in times of stress, the following circumstances might trigger the inferior function:

- When people close to them deny verifiable facts and givens in a situation, act on impractical ideas or in inappropriate ways, or overrule common sense.
- When there is no clear sense of direction in the midst of change. ISFJs work to smooth transitions and are vexed when plans can't be made.
- When future outcomes are unclear or the situation is taken out of their hands. ISFJs can easily dwell on worst-case scenarios.
- When they go too far in deferring their own needs to meet those of others.

For my husband's job, we moved our family ten times in twenty years, first across the United States and then to Europe. I always wanted to put down roots—especially to be near my mother and the town where I was raised—but the chance came too late. For consolation at the time, I read and studied the life of Sarah, Abraham's wife. You know,

Sarah had her problems and things did not work out her way, yet she was a survivor. I know I'm a survivor, too.
—Elisabeth, 67, homemaker

Often, the worst times for ISFJs come in the midst of change when they cannot identify a clear, understandable course of action. As they focus on what needs to be done to get through each day, their attention may be drawn away from the overall awareness of how problematic the situation really is.

> *During the divorce process, I kept my attention on all the details and on my children. Only after the divorce was final could I really see how awful our marriage had been. I have to get through a loss experience before I can evaluate it in a larger perspective. Then I can be more realistic.*
> —Greg, 46, customer service manager

In these situations, ISFJs might express excessive pessimism and forebodings about the future. They might also obsess on what they see as the givens, the things they can't change, to the extent that they cannot think through alternatives. When these symptoms appear, a totally different approach to soulwork often helps. ISFJs might *purposefully* pursue Extraverted Intuition, talking with others or looking to the outside world for new ideas. Its *conscious use* requires the ISFJ to shut down what is usually easiest—Introverted Sensing—which may have gotten out of control. By doing so, the ISFJ can add new information to their ponderings, opening up different solutions or strategies.

Ways to consciously engage the Intuitive function include

- taking a negative situation and thinking of at least three positives that could come from it. Or, considering the most terrible thing that could happen and figuring out how to deal with the worst-case scenario to break the logjam of gloomy thinking.
- asking questions about the who-what-when-where-why-how of the current and future state of affairs, then discussing with friends to determine what it all means in the larger context of life.
- engaging in a creative activity such as art, writing, or woodworking, where there is no pressure to produce a specific outcome, giving over to the process of seeing who or what else emerges.

In the chosen activity, the key is to move past the boundaries of the ISFJ's own thoughts and experiences, gaining new insights from diverse ideas and opinions. An ISFJ explains, "I get so locked in to my fears—as when my sister died. We'd been so close; I couldn't imagine life without her. I sank into depression, wouldn't leave the house. Then a friend reminded me, 'There *is* a heaven. You'll be together there.' I'd lost sight of that straightforward truth until her sincerity brought my thoughts back into balance."

As an ISFJ, I am thankful for
>my practical outlook, which sees things as they truly are;
>my sense of duty, service, and responsibility;
>the fulfillment I feel when I have helped another;
>the beauty of nature and the company of friends.

When life is difficult, I can find support by
>finding a listening friend who can act as a compass as I try out new directions,
>broadening my perspective through reading sacred texts and the testimonies of others who faced similar circumstances,
>appreciating and honoring my own needs, talents, and gifts.

To honor myself and my pathway to God, I can
>seek quiet times for reflection and relaxation,
>use my imagination to open my spiritual practices to the richness in life that exists beyond the tangible and concrete,
>invest time with God, knowing God is in control and therefore I don't have to be.

The Paths of Intuitive Spirituality

The imagination is the secret and marrow of civilization. It is the very eye of faith. The soul without imagination is what an observatory would be without a telescope.[1]

—Henry Ward Beecher

Intuitive types find satisfying soulwork through
- living the spiritual life with optimism and hope;
- enjoying insights, imagination, creativity, novelty, for things seen and unseen;
- appreciating and contemplating the inexplicable and the mystical aspects of life;
- seeing applications for future possibilities, meaning, growth, and change;
- learning through synchronistic interaction between ideas, occurrences, people, and scholarship;
- observing meanings and connections behind the events, stories, or practices of spirituality;
- designing new avenues, traditions, or rituals for soulwork.

Preferred Extraverted Intuitive Soulwork (Ch. 5: ENTP and ENFP)	Preferred Introverted Intuitive Soulwork (Ch. 6: INTJ and INFJ)
• Prayer or meditation in community	• Prayer or meditation in solitude
• Soulwork through interaction with others and the environment to enhance the future	• Soulwork through musing with God about what could be different or might be in store
• Spontaneous spiritual life, as perceptions or needs arise	• Structured and special times set apart expressly for spiritual matters
• Service through actions to make things better for people, organizations, or the natural world	• Service through conceiving paradigms, envisioning and organizing the structures for change

Suggestions for Intuitive Spirituality

1. Choose a favorite story that has meaning for you spiritually. It could be from the writings of your spiritual heritage, an oft-told tale about an ancestor, a person you admire, or a fictional character. Imagine yourself as a character in the story or reconsider the plot, lesson to be learned, or causes of what occurred. What new insights do you receive? What new messages are there for you in the story?

2. Henry David Thoreau said, "The youth gets together his materials to build a bridge to the moon, or, perchance, a palace or temple on the earth, and, at length, the middle-aged man concludes to build a woodshed with them."[2]

   • In what areas of your life have you built woodsheds instead of palaces?

   • What could you change to recover your dream?

3. Change the patterns of your soulwork frequently. Read different inspirational texts, take a different route on your walk, set aside a spiritual practice or discipline before it becomes too boring. Find ways to use your imagination to support your soulwork:

   • Picture a future event and the outcomes you hope will occur.

   • Bring to mind a person and the change or blessings you would like to see for that person.

   • Imagine the results of changes you hope to see in yourself.

   • Place yourself in the presence of your Creator. What messages might you receive? What lessons are you to learn?

   • Create in your mind an image of joy, calm, repentance—whatever your greatest need at the moment—and envision what life would or could be like.

4. For the discipline of simplicity: The minds of many Intuitive types are easily distracted from soulwork. What are your major distractions? Involvement in too many good causes? Interest in too many subjects? Reading too many "informative" magazines or too much time surfing the Internet? If less is more, then imagine what your work, family, emotional well-being, and leisure time might gain from ridding yourself of some of these distractions and adding time for soulwork.

5. For the discipline of celebration: Rejoice in your creativity. Devote time to your novel ideas, your music, your art, your writing, your

designing—whatever the gifts God gave to you. Allow yourself opportunities, alone or with others, to browse at a bookstore, visit an art museum, or attend a concert, thankful for the insights you receive. Use your creativity to celebrate and offer thanksgiving—make cards instead of buying them, designate certain foods or table settings as festival items, invite friends for an evening of games, indulge in a walk in the middle of a day, even turn the music up a bit louder.

6. Think of or journal about three people in your life who encouraged you. What did they see as your future? What did they think you did well? How could their dreams or insights about you help you now? Or, imagine yourself as a young person. From your adult perspective, what do you view as your own potential? What can you do to bring that potential forward into the future?

7. If time and money were no object (and after the trip around the world!), what would you attempt to do or be? Envision yourself carrying out your dream. What would it be like? How would it fulfill you? How can you incorporate steps toward that fulfillment into your life right now?

8. Envision yourself ten or twenty years from now. Will you be pleased with what you are doing or whom you have become? If so, what do you need to do *now* to make your future a reality? If not, how can you work to modify your life now? How do you think your future self would regard your current activities?

9. Allow yourself at least thirty minutes alone with music that calls to your soul—consider making a tape of favorite songs just for your listening pleasure. Sit back with your journal, art, clay, tablet, computer (or walk with a set of headphones) and let the music inspire you.

10. Remember that as an Intuitive type, daydreams can be rich areas for insights. Even as you daydream, pretend that you are discussing your ideas with God. Don't immediately censor "wild thoughts." What might God be trying to suggest? Are you open to discoveries in this manner? What are your longings? How could these longings be the voice of your soul?

Extraverted Intuitive Soulwork

1. With whom do you share your dreams and disappointments? Is there someone who will be trustworthy yet will challenge you if needed? Risk sharing your ideas for growth and change. As you converse, how do you feel? Excited? Confident? How can this person serve as a springboard to help you to make your dreams become reality?

2. For the discipline of study: Imagine that you could invite any three spiritual giants to serve on a panel for discussion. Whom would you invite? What would you want to ask them? What could you explore together? What might you hope to discover? How could they be a stimulus for your soulwork?

3. For the discipline of prayer: If your soulwork becomes too incidental or accidental, try using meditative resources to bring specific actions for soulwork to fruition. Use an object or picture for meditation to anchor your thoughts. Perhaps placing an icon or sacred object on your dresser, in your billfold, or by your desk could serve to remind you to meditate or pray.

4. In what type of environment do you really dream best? At the seashore? By a favorite window? In a bookstore? On a walk in nature? Driving or biking through a pleasant scene? When were you last there?

    Go to one of these spots today and be conscious of what happens. What insights did you receive for your work? Your relationships? Your soulwork? How can you make more time for this essential soulwork?

    If you can't go to your sacred spot regularly, recreate it in your mind. Picture the journey there, the sights, sounds, and smells, and what you would do along the way and once you arrive. Allow yourself time to be in these environments so that you can access your spiritual potential.

Introverted Intuitive Soulwork

1. When did you last play the piano, play the guitar, play the flute, sing, dance, sculpt, or something similar? For many Introverted Intuitive types, these activities can be a major source of peace and renewal. Use these activities and others like them as ways to inspire your soulwork.

2. Who are your favorite spiritual heroes? What about them inspires you? Read enough about them so that you can imagine the realities of their day-to-day living and perhaps find new meaning in their writings or deeds. In what context did their insights come? How is your life similar to theirs? What can you do to emulate them?

3. For the discipline of study: Go steep and deep with a short passage from your sacred texts, favorite poems, or teachings from someone you admire. Understand the facts the passage presents, but then look for other meanings and interpretations. Stick with the same reading until you garner new insights. When you have gained new awareness, consider the truth of your ideas and the impact they might have on you or others.

4. For the discipline of prayer: If your soulwork becomes too incidental or accidental, try using meditative resources to bring specific actions for soulwork to fruition. Keep lists of petitions and praise in a notebook. Decide on a format for prayer; include set supplications or readings and other reminders to keep your soulwork focused.

CHAPTER FIVE

EXTRAVERTED INTUITION:

The Catalytic Spiritual Path

Extraverted Intuitive Spirituality
ENTP, ENFP

Seeking possibilities.
Exploring different forms of soulwork.
Crafting new ideas for uplifting human aspirations
or creative solutions to the world's problems.

"Spiritual *practices?*" an Extraverted Intuitive type commented to us. "I'm an information junkie, always looking for novel ways that people pursue spirituality. You might say I collect religious traditions—it's the practicing of those traditions I tend to forget!"

Extraverted Intuitive spirituality is a continual search for philosophies, exploring the inexplicable, experiencing the new or unfamiliar, all in the quest for deeper understanding. Some Extraverted Intuitives maintain that they are perpetual seekers who hesitate to choose a single spiritual path simply because too many possibilities exist—too many ways of knowing. Others, with their affinity for the unseen, find the concept of God to be an essential one, settling within one tradition, yet continually looking for new ways to enrich their soulwork.

> *My upbringing didn't include any religious tradition, so I had none to overcome! However, as a young adult when my life wasn't working the way I wanted it to, my natural curiosity sent me searching for what was missing.*
>
> *I learned about soulwork and found that I enjoyed being with others I viewed as spiritual. I can see the positive results of people of faith in action. However, I'm still searching—any God worthy of the name can handle my inclination to check on other possibilities!*
> —Paula, 48, human resources manager

Extraverted Intuitive types may craft their own fluid belief system with information from many sources. Their spirituality responds to new and changing insights, like a mobile that changes direction with varying movements of air. While others may see this as fickle, amidst the changes is a bedrock of values and principles centered on discovering meaning and purpose for themselves and others.

While many Extraverted Intuitive types have a natural distrust of rigid structures or hierarchies, they often seek out spiritual communities for the relationships they can develop there. These group experiences provide avenues for richness and variety in soulwork. Their most spiritual times tend to be inspired by interactions with other people or stimuli from the world around them. In essence, their soulwork fuels self-identity as a foundation for making a difference in the world, whether in their immediate circle of influence or on a larger scale.

> *When I joined the Al-Anon 12-Step Program, I found such a serenity that I felt compelled to reach out to people who struggle with addictions and the accompanying loss of hope. By following the Al-Anon philosophy of putting my issues into God's hands—you know, "Let go, let God"—I reached a peace I never thought possible.*
> —Barbara, 53, publicist

For Extraverted Intuitive types, openness in faith and practice is essential; beliefs should be explored and examined before being accepted. As they look for fellowship, they need to know that individual perspectives are valued. They may also branch out to dialogue with those with very different traditions and understandings.

Extraverted Intuitive types often move outward to lead or encourage others, especially through speaking, teaching, performing, or taking charge of new endeavors. They may assume those roles through a variety of paths inside or outside of traditional religion by leading organizations or support groups, by teaching academic classes or informal seminars, and by writing or speaking.

> *As a child, my spirituality was connected with my desire to help others. My imagination allowed me to put myself in the shoes of people who struggled in poverty. I wanted to be a part of efforts to help them— either in person or by leading "crusades" to save the world from strife and hunger. Now I believe my insights and concerns for people are the gifts of God that enable me to look beyond myself. While I'm not the global crusader of my childhood dreams, through my profession, I restore people one at a time.*
> —Nan, 62, therapist

Spirituality for Extraverted Intuitive types, then, often serves as motivation for becoming catalysts for change—in themselves, in others, and in the injustices of the world. They are often more attracted to active soul-work, whether through dialogue, actions, or gathering with others, than to more staid or solitary practices.

Prayer

At its best, Extraverted Intuitive prayer involves imagination and input from the outside world. While some find it advantageous to hold themselves to a set prayer time each day, lest their typical whirlwind of activities crowd it out all together, most find a spontaneous prayer life most satisfying.

- Extraverted Intuitive types might feel compelled to talk with their Creator while viewing a piece of art, listening to music, witnessing an act of kindness, or experiencing a wonder in nature.
- They might join with others for regular prayer. Sharing their own joys and burdens, while in turn supporting others, adds vitality to their prayer lives.
- Rather than following a set schedule or ritual for prayer, Extraverted Intuitive types might arrange their environment to more regularly

spark prayer. They might look at their weekly calendar and schedule time for reflection at a local arboretum. They might make time for a monthly "mini retreat," simply turning off phones and contemplating the events of the past weeks. They might also place physical reminders on their dresser, dashboard, or above the kitchen sink to remind them of people they wish to support in prayer.

An icon of Mary holding Jesus after he was taken down from the cross sits on my dresser. Whenever I view it I say a prayer for my son who struggles with mental illness. It reminds me that I've consistently done all that I can for him. Like Mary, I had to turn my son over to God while still praying and being there for him.
  —Jasmine, 56, corporate trainer

- Enriching prayer might also come through engaging the imagination or through novel approaches. Some Extraverted Intuitive types use guided imagery to reflect on what is missing in their lives or to gain insights into their hopes, disappointments, or uncertainties. They might frequently attend workshops, retreats, classes, or read books to find new, creative ways of tapping into prayer.

I'm interested in anything spiritual that has helped others. I may not make it a regular part of my soulwork, but I don't like to feel that I may have overlooked a resource.
  —Deanna, 55, professor

Worship

For worship, Extraverted Intuitive types embrace the possibilities and the energy that come with exploring the sacred in community. Atmospheres with a touch of festive celebration often feed their souls.

- Many Extraverted Intuitive types gain enthusiasm and feel a sense of being connected with a bigger purpose from participating in formal worship gatherings. Music, engaging stories, drama, and other artistic expressions often fuel the imaginative side of their spiritual journeys.
- They enjoy variety and spontaneity in worship. If a place of worship offers more than one style of service, Extraverted Intuitive types might have a favorite but may also vary which one they

attend, depending on their mood or needs. They may also be drawn to planning or assisting with new litanies, worship formats, or avenues for corporate prayer.

While I usually enjoy our church's hand-clapping, energetic contemporary service, some weeks make me long for soulful rather than spirit-filled worship. Then I attend the quieter evening service. The candles, the organ, the soloists allow me to talk with God about what I've been experiencing rather than celebrate as if life is perfect.
    —Alex, 50, school choir director

- Extraverted Intuitive types find that sermons or other teachings hold their attention when they help them envision new possibilities or provide unique metaphors they can apply to understanding different situations.

Study

Extraverted Intuitive types often prefer to know something about many things rather than a lot about just a few things, seeking breadth instead of depth. Driven by their curiosity, their study of soulwork can take many forms.

- Many Extraverted Intuitive types gravitate to formal education and may seek university or seminary classes to learn more about their faith.
- To learn, they may read broadly or research topics that are of particular interest to them.
- Extraverted Intuitive types also often enjoy free-ranging discussions with others, exploring the intersection of spiritual concerns with personal or worldly concerns. They hope to gain from others' experiences, background, and knowledge.

When I see the positive results of faith in action, I'm able to halt my analysis of spirituality and engage my intuition to imagine how soulwork can change things. There are enough ideas out there that my frame of reference is slowly shifting from doubt to belief.
    —Andrew, 38, marketing representative

Service

Extraverted Intuitive types often hope that by tapping into their spiritual motivations, people can band together to change the world, or at least one aspect of it at a time. With their enthusiasm and frequent ability to influence others, Extraverted Intuitive types often bring their ideas to fruition.

- Extraverted Intuitive types may participate in humanitarian projects where they feel they can have an impact, perhaps by orchestrating refugee relief, managing teen mission trips, or raising funds. Or they find themselves in other leadership roles where they can direct efforts in new and uncharted waters.

  While chaperoning a youth ski trip, I became so frustrated with the lack of planning and coordination that I took on the responsibility of running the trips for the next couple of years. I could see what needed to be planned and enlisted help to manage the details. Then my intuition kicked in for the unexpected happenings—like being stranded in the middle of Nebraska by a blizzard!
  —Drew, 55, consultant

- Task forces or committees that work to change the status quo or plan for the future are other natural avenues for service.

  I generally end up in leadership positions. At times I have felt like the true pioneer, musket balls in my rear from getting too far ahead of the troops—perceived as the enemy rather than the visionary.
  —Hans, 61, small-business owner

- Many Extraverted Intuitive types seek opportunities to help others experience connections and personal growth. They might pursue careers in counseling, human resources, or social work where they can directly help people in need or influence organizations to serve people better.

Other Forms of Soulwork

With their endless curiosity, Extraverted Intuitive types find endless ways to tap into their spiritual side by joining with others or seeking out the infinite varieties of soulwork practiced around the world, in different cultures, or through enriching and changing the traditions of their own faith.

- Extraverted Intuitive types often travel, attend local classes, or participate in retreats with others to experience, not just read about, different cultural and spiritual traditions. They often seek to find points of agreement between these and their own tradition as well as common patterns or threads they might explore.
- They might read novels or biographies, or watch movies, and then gather with friends to discuss resulting insights into spirituality or life's struggles.

I can scarcely see a play, read a book, or watch the news without finding a spiritual connection—to me, almost every joy or tragedy is best viewed through the lens of my faith. What would I have done? What would God want me to do as a friend, neighbor, or counsel to those involved? Should I be living differently? Can I use the story as an illustration for a class I'm teaching? The list is endless.
—Dave, 45, minister

- Extraverted Intuitive types' soulwork may also focus on determining a philosophy that allows them to synthesize life's blessings and tragedies.

I was only seven years old when, in the space of a few months, three children in our neighborhood died. The uncertainty of life was underscored in a way that was far beyond my maturity to grasp, but I understood that in some ways and aspects of life, things were beyond my control. No matter how gifted I was in matters of the mind (I was already the best reader in class), body (a natural athlete), and heart (I had many friends), I knew that life was still like water—you couldn't hold it in your hands. I knew I had to find something deeper, what I now refer to as my soul, to guide me through life.
—Craig, 48, strategic planning consultant

In short, Extraverted Intuitive spirituality helps all of us remember that

- spirituality can be a lifelong adventure;
- different ideas fuel questions and aid us in affirming what we believe;
- variety in soulwork keeps us from slipping into unthinking practices;

- journeying together adds energy, ideas, and the power of what groups can accomplish when they combine efforts.

The Second Half of Life's Spiritual Journey

While Extraverted Intuition is about exploration and possibilities, eventually life grows short. Or, as do all personalities, the Extraverted Intuitive types begin to wonder whether they have found sufficient meaning and purpose. If they continue on their current path, will they regret not enjoying the present moment?

Often at this stage, the Extraverted Intuitive types have developed their spiritual path. Then, richness comes through the inferior function, Introverted Sensing. This involves

- structured time for reflective spiritual discipline to focus on depth and clarity of understanding;
- using the five senses—what can be seen, heard, touched, smelled, or tasted—to enrich soulwork;
- applying spirituality to practical, personal needs;
- reflecting on or participating in the continuity of traditions or rituals that have stood the test of time.

While Extraverted Intuitive types may continue many of their favorite methods of soulwork, here are some examples of what they found as they journeyed on into Sensing:

I'm dedicating two mornings a week to quiet reading and journaling. I enjoy it so much that I may just add a third morning! When I still myself to listen, my quietude brings me blessings. I can rest in just being, instead of always doing.

The trappings of my spiritual life are now important. Give me something that I can see, smell, or touch! I like candles, music, and other things that call my senses to notice what is spiritual. Maybe I overdid the deep symbolism—now I'm seeing simple things as miracles. Lying in the grass and feeling its softness frees my mind of ideas and brings out my emotions of gladness and gratitude at the splendor of what actually is. Who says this is the "inferior function"!

Preparing the Sabbath meal in the traditional way gives me a sense of the rhythm of my weeks—something I previously overlooked in my busy life. Small disciplines practiced routinely bring me contentment in a way that my haphazard practices did not. The discipline of the Sabbath arrangements and its meaning for our family make me focus on one thing—seeing God in the everyday events of life.

Alone during prayer, I often become flooded with joy for my own physical being. I do yoga now, too. Honoring my physical body in all its wonder is a significant way of doing soulwork. I breathe, I feel my own body and become concretely aware of the beauty and mystery of life—I am alive!

I enjoy going back over my childhood and early adult years to reflect on how my spiritual life has developed. This practice reminds me where I've been and how that influences what is meaningful for me. I may be back where I started. I want to enjoy the stage I'm at and not worry about what comes next.

I was in a leadership meeting last week. As the group struggled to define, What is it that we are supposed to "get" in our spiritual community? a good friend, the quietest person there, said, "It's about joy." That's where I hope my journey takes me.

Any of the Sensing pathways (chapters 3 and 4) can bring this kind of rest and richness for Extraverted Intuitive types if they allow their dominant Extraverted Intuition function a time of rest and let the Spirit guide their thoughts and actions.

ENTP

Extraversion Intuition Thinking Perceiving

Spirituality in the outer world of challenges and possibilities

> *Not that I have already obtained this or have already reached the goal; but I press on to make it my own, because Christ Jesus has made me his own.*
> —*Philippians 3:12,* NRSV

Greatest Gifts

Conceptualizing what needs to be by integrating divergent ideas; Bringing insight to complex and challenging situations to overcome obstacles

Role in Community

Planning and leading new projects with enthusiasm and energy; Assuming the risks for visionary endeavors; Advocating strategies for the future

ENTPs tend to be independent innovators and change masters. They enjoy originality of expression, questioning ideas and norms, and developing models. ENTPs follow their hunches and investigate new, intriguing possibilities for systems and organizations. The call of adventure, allowing for freedom of action, entices ENTPs.

Using their dominant function, Extraverted Intuition, is the natural starting place for soulwork. However, their auxiliary or second function, *Introverted Thinking*, calls them to pull back for reflection and logical analysis.

Soulwork through the Second Function

Through Introverted Thinking, ENTPs can work to add logic and structure to all the ideas that flood their minds and their interactions with others. ENTPs often have so many irons in the fire that they struggle to find this introspective time. They may need to intentionally withdraw from their normal environments to reflect on their experiences.

> *The situation with my daughter and her boyfriend was so crazy that it was driving me wild. I decided to get away for the day, so I rented a rowboat. I found a secluded inlet where no one could see me and spent several hours just being still to sort things out and decide on a course of action.*
> —Jeff, 50, sales executive

ENTPs can also access their introverted Thinking by setting aside time for meditation, prayer, or reading. Learning to say no and sticking with it can give ENTPs this quiet time and perhaps the opportunity to complete those projects they always wanted to finish.

ENTPs might access Introverted Thinking using any of the Thinking exercises on pages 145-149, with goals such as

- focusing their spirituality on their own principles and needs;
- developing systems for prioritization and purpose to determine which of their many interests have the most merit;
- defining for themselves what is true and relevant;
- adding discipline to their search through meditation, organized study, or writing to rethink what is true;
- choosing objectively among the many options they perceive.

All of these might help them bring clarity to their beliefs and depth to their soulwork.

> *My most helpful spiritual director brought a group of us together weekly to teach us how to "reflect"—no easy matter for someone who wants to constantly be part of the action. Even though the director moved away, our group still meets. I need the encouragement of others to pull back and clarify what I believe.*
> —Paige, 51, attorney

What Might Push ENTPs Away from Their Spiritual Path

With the entire world beckoning and their general sense of urgency and competency, many ENTPs struggle to make room for soulwork. Common themes we heard from the people we interviewed included

- being led by their own intuitive drive to want to know about *all* different types of spirituality and therefore never choosing one.
- having concerns about how others view religion and their "need" for it. They don't want anyone to question their intellect. If ENTPs are still exploring his or her spirituality and haven't developed a deep enough understanding to feel competent, his or her self-doubt can become a spiritual conundrum. Further, judgmental surroundings can block their search. If they *do* persevere, sometimes ENTPs' natural questioning style, driving for truth and clarity, can be viewed by the "faithful" as challenging rather than curious.

    I talk a good game about not caring what others think of me, and in the majority of areas of life this is true. But I never wanted anyone to question my intellect—and this is my spiritual "Catch 22." I want that absolute freedom from care that my perception of true faith brings, but I have to make myself vulnerable to do that.
    —Sachi, 33, corporate trainer

- seeing little need to pursue soulwork, given ENTPs' customary self-confidence. Often only after some adversity or hard-to-master challenge do they develop a more spiritual rather than intellectual point of view. These difficult situations become the spurs for them to look more deeply at who or what outside of themselves could provide strength.
- not finding time for soulwork. With all of the areas for exploration that ENTPs find through their Intuition, they tend not to make space for spirituality unless it is particularly compelling or their life circumstances overwhelm their usual optimism. Then they might look outside themselves for help.

Trusted spiritual advisors, friends, and family can help ENTPs find an enriching spiritual path by

- not overselling the benefits of a spiritual life, letting the ENTPs come at it on their own terms;

- reminding them that they did their best in a given situation and that effort, not perfection, is sometimes the better yardstick;
- engaging with them in a deep enough relationship for sharing problems;
- sustaining their faith by sharing stories of people who experienced serious problems and survived.

When Life Is Difficult

The fourth, or *inferior,* function for ENTPs is Introverted Sensing. With their emphasis on possibilities, tapping into the Introverted Sensing realm of facts and details to deal with the present moment is a struggle. In times of stress, the inferior function can erupt, changing their behavior into a caricature of ISFJs and ISTJs for whom it is the *dominant* function.

For ENTPs in times of stress, the following circumstances might trigger the inferior function:

- When they continue to attack a problem long after others would admit defeat. Many ENTPs have little experience with anything that they cannot conquer using their own power. Because of their dauntless ingenuity and energy, ENTPs often manage to avoid some of life's setbacks and therefore sometimes do not recognize the severity of their dilemma.
- When they need to deal with emotion-laden, personal issues. ENTPs prefer to avoid showing the emotional side of themselves or to experience that vulnerability in others.
- When they are asked to follow standard operating procedures that truly get in the way of what they are trying to accomplish or that violate one of their core principles.
- When they feel that they are being unfairly challenged, especially in areas where they perceive they have a corner on the truth. Because they strive to be experts in their areas of interest, they can be particularly unnerved when people question their competency or uncover details they have overlooked.

The worst times for ENTPs often are when they are forced to give up, admitting that their resourcefulness and genuine optimism cannot handle the crisis. Perhaps they overused their dominant function, assuming that once again they could generate options until something worked.

For the first few years of dealing with our child's health issues, we kept the matter pretty much to ourselves. I read every book I could find until it seemed that sometimes I knew more than the specialists. When the doctors began to hint that there were no further options, I felt as if I had somehow betrayed my daughter. If I'd put more energy into other strategies or moved our family to be nearer to a research hospital, etc., I might have licked the problem. My mind kept dwelling on what I could have done to find a cure for her—a pretty futile task.
—Shari, 48, lobbyist

In these situations, ENTPs might overindulge in sensory pursuits by overeating, sleeping too much, exercising excessively, or watching mindless television. They may also resist any challenge, no matter how grounded in facts, to their course of action or understanding of events. When these symptoms appear, a totally different approach to soulwork often helps. ENTPs might *purposefully* pursue Introverted Sensing. Its *conscious use* requires the ENTP to shut down what is usually easiest—Extraverted Intuition—which may have gotten out of control. By doing so, the ENTP can slow down to concentrate and focus on the facts and the needs of the present moment.

Ways to consciously engage the Sensing function include:

- Practicing meditation or other solitary disciplines to pay attention to the internal world. Mindful meditation can provide benefits without adding yet another burdensome activity to their hectic schedule. Time alone in reflection or prayer with concentrated attention on breathing and thought patterns can be a balm to the often-dispersed ENTP.

- Using images of nature to calm the soul. While some ENTPs seek solitude outside, others imagine favorite places. One ENTP quiets herself by picturing in her mind a storm-swept lake, the feel of the biting wind, the sounds of crashing waves, the smell of rain, and then gradually imagines the storm subsiding until the lake is as still as glass.

- Engaging in exercise, massage, and other types of bodywork can help ENTPs relax, appreciate their physical strengths and limitations, and regain balance.

In the chosen activity, the key is backing away from defeat or despair and attending to present needs. One ENTP reflected, "God is that voice within that I 'hear' when I'm in a sanctuary or that place between sleep and wakefulness or wherever I'm still enough to listen. Being quiet brings blessings!"

As an ENTP, I am thankful for

my energy and enthusiasm for life's challenges,

my creative and innovative vision,

my ability to see patterns and find solutions,

the way I can synthesize divergent ideas.

When life is difficult, I can find support by

prioritizing my many options and concluding which best meet my life principles,

cutting out distractions and allowing space for reflection and solitude,

paying attention to and living within those rules and guidelines that I know are important to me.

To honor myself and my pathway to God, I can

seek answers, question the pat solutions, and discover the spiritual truths of this world;

pay attention to *what is* and value reality for the evidence and richness it brings to my spiritual journey;

dedicate time for my spiritual practices and life.

ENFP

Extraversion Intuition
Feeling Perceiving

*Spirituality in the outer world of
activities and possibilities for people*

---

*Whatever is true, whatever is noble, whatever is right, whatever is pure,
whatever is lovely, whatever is admirable—if anything is excellent or praise-
worthy—think about such things.*
—Philippians 4:8

Greatest Gifts
Generating numerous ideas and finding abundant resources; Finding
enjoyment in an infinite variety of interests; Aligning passion and creativity in the processes of discovery, learning, and living

Role in Community
Inspiring others to reach their fullest potential; Building generous and
open communities to help in the advancement of worthwhile causes and
the shepherding of human aspirations

ENFPs tend to be enthusiastic, inspiring, and charismatic initiators
of change who value exploring possibilities for growth and development.
Energetic and perceptive, ENFPs often anticipate what people will want in
the future. They enjoy variety, newness, and flexibility. Creativity, novelty,
and insight are key values.

Using their dominant function, Extraverted Intuition, is the natural
starting place for soulwork. However, their auxiliary or second function,

---

Introverted Feeling, calls them to pull back from their active lifestyle to reflect on what is important.

Soulwork through the Second Function

For ENFPs, space and time spent alone allows them to find the balance that their second function of Introverted Feeling can provide, offering an internal sense of support or an inner awareness that they are not alone. Going on a retreat, if only to spend a few *quiet* hours in nature, may give ENFPs time to reflect on their inner emotional state. Introverted Feeling can also help add structure or discipline to their soulwork. They may turn to reading, prayer, or meditation more regularly. Reviewing past journal entries serves to remind ENFPs where they have stumbled before, what helped them, and how they have grown.

> *When my business failed, I couldn't sleep past five in the morning. I started using that time for journaling and meditation. I know that "still, small voice" speaks to me only when I stop the chase, quiet down, and listen. Now, even though such discipline on my part is a challenge, life seems easier when I start my day with the grounding that comes from listening for God.*
> —Devon, 43, consultant

Cutting back on activities, amusements, or other external pulls is another way to slow the pace and create a space for soulwork. Learning to say no to the requests of others—particularly hard for ENFPs because they may seek to be all things to all people—can also supply some time, even if it is *only* for rest.

Through journaling, prayer, or meditation, ENFPs might use any of the Introverted Feeling exercises (pages 193-198) to

- determine needs and priorities for themselves and others close to them,
- develop a rationale for reducing or eliminating some of the activities that crowd their lives,
- assess their own inner emotional state,
- clarify whether their values are congruent with a situation or an opportunity,
- consider whether they have said yes to so many obligations or opportunities that they may not be able to meet all of them.

All of these might help them bring clarity to their beliefs and depth to their soulwork.

> *When I learned that others would respect my needs and still love me, I felt a great sense of relief about saying no. I discovered that many requests can be satisfied by other people or resources. Giving myself time and nourishment makes it even more viable for me to offer spiritual and emotional support to others.*
> —Sara, 50, sales manager

What Might Push ENFPs Away from Their Spiritual Path

With their openness to many forms of soulwork and their enthusiasm for so many aspects of life, several factors can keep an ENFP from their spiritual pursuits. Common themes we heard from the people we interviewed included

- being pulled by too many facets of life. ENFPs often struggle to balance their physical, emotional, and spiritual needs because their Extraverted Intuition constantly beckons with possibilities of new treasures. Busyness then interferes with their need for soulwork.
- becoming bored by familiar spiritual practices. During routine services or rituals ENFPs may find that their minds wander and soulwork loses its appeal.

> *Rote readings, liturgies, and prayers make me feel fidgety. I often tune out traditional language and predictable practices just because they are predictable. They don't touch a deep chord.*
> —Neil, 42, marketing representative

- burning out through over-involvement. ENFPs may readily volunteer to support causes or new spiritual practices, beliefs, or leaders. Often before they realize it, they are overextended, feeling guilty, and burned out. Things begin to slip through the cracks. Then they may withdraw or resign to bring their lives back under control, only to start this process over again.
- knowing they may find many conflicting systems of belief. ENFPs may avoid a typically spiritual life because they may not want to face the potential for conflict and apparent incongruities of their own beliefs and those of others.

Trusted spiritual advisors, friends, and family can help ENFPs find an enriching spiritual path by

- allowing for doubt and ambiguity. God seems absent when rules or judgments are too heavy-handed.
- helping them concentrate on the meaning of faith in its *daily* applications, forcing them to slow down to pay attention to spiritual and physical needs.
- sharing their deeply held spiritual values and moments of grace.
- acting as "family," showing care and concern in times of crisis.

When Life Is Difficult

The fourth, or *inferior,* function for ENFPs is Introverted Sensing. With their emphasis on everything that is out there and endless possibilities, tapping into the Introverted Sensing realm of immediate details and needs is a struggle. In times of stress, the inferior function can erupt, changing the ENFP's behavior into a caricature of ISTJs and ISFJs for whom it is the *dominant* function.

For ENFPs in times of stress, the following circumstances might trigger the inferior function:

- When problems cause them to focus primarily on the facts involved, especially if they need to make immediate decisions. Because ENFPs' attention is oriented toward the big picture, they would rather procrastinate than attend to the unvarnished reality and details of an impending or immediate crisis.

  I was just about to leave on a pilgrimage when I found out I was diabetic and needed to immediately start a restricted diet. Deciding whether or not to go put me in a real quandary because I wasn't sure that the foods I needed would be available. I changed my mind several times over—my body seemed at war with my soul. I was depressed, totally locked in by the reality of my illness. My despair at being diabetic and its reality of a possible reduction in my activities took me by surprise.
  —Sonja, 51, human resources professional

- When they lose track of the important while trying to cope with the urgent, leaving them without a sense of purpose. ENFPs can become stressed when they realize how much there is to do and how little time or energy they have to do it. If a crisis requires a barrage of activity, they may get caught up in the frenzy and not give time to their souls.

- When a loss of personal relationship seems inevitable or final.
- When they are forced to face a tragedy *alone,* either physically or emotionally. ENFPs can find being alone with their problems quite depressing. While most ENFPs have circles of support, those who are without close family or friends to fully share their burdens can feel overwhelmed and alone.

Often, the worst times for ENFPs are when all options seem to be closed and all resources are exhausted—a "no way out" situation or a lose-lose scenario. The finality and certainty of some life events challenge their sunny optimism. Then they may obsess on finding the newest, latest, or most attractive alternative. If none of these works, ENFPs hit bottom.

> *Looking back, I can't believe I was so oblivious to how overly committed I was, but it took a major auto accident to bring me to my senses. The accident was a direct result of trying to be two places at the same time, skidding out in the snow by driving too fast. Lying in the hospital after reconstructive facial surgery, I had a lot of time to introspect. No career was worth the time I'd been spending away from my family, friends, and God. I vowed to make some changes in my priorities. I wrote down my values and commitments. Now every few months I review these to see whether my life is on track with these values.*
> —Callie, 37, consultant

In these situations, ENFPs might sink into depression, losing their normally positive outlook. They can obsess over a health concern, convinced that they have a serious or terminal illness. They might also become obsessed with typically overlooked physical details. When these symptoms appear, a totally different approach to soulwork often helps. ENFPs might *purposely* pursue Introverted Sensing. Its *conscious use* requires the ENFP to shut down what is usually easiest—Extraverted Intuition—which may have gotten out of control. By doing so, the ENFP can slow down to concentrate on what can be done in the moment to help the situation.

Ways to consciously engage the Sensing function include

- giving regular time to soulwork through meditation, yoga, or other pursuits that require mental absorption and therefore help clear the mind of clutter and chatter.

- pampering the body with massage, relaxing baths, regular and strenuous exercise, or other practices where the focus is on tangible physical needs.
- concentrating on the immediate impact of the situation: emotions, health, fatigue, and the like. By assessing what is *really* happening, not what they want to have happen, ENFPs can take necessary steps to reduce their stress.

I need to take time to pay attention to my body. This information brings incredible insights about how I truly feel about a person, job, or situation—if I get a headache after an encounter with someone, I use that data to consider what in the relationship is stressful to me.
　　—Rosa, 60, adult educator

In the chosen activity, the key is to focus on reality through sensory data, the facts, and the details until a new pathway to peace is found. One ENFP said, "Remaining in the present—paying close attention to myself, the situation, and others—while letting the past go and the future take care of itself has opened a special kind of serenity for me."

As an ENFP, I am thankful for
my enthusiasm for all the wonderful possibilities that exist in the world,
my imagination and insights,
my resourcefulness and optimism,
my emphasis on striving to be all I can be.

When life is difficult, I can find support by
quieting down, removing the busy distractions from my life;
allowing myself to rest to nurture my soul;
focusing on what is truly of value to me.

To honor myself and my pathway to God, I can
give free reign to my imagination as I find creative options for soul-work,
develop my own spiritual philosophy from the many avenues I explore,
carve out small amounts of time alone for reflection or prayer to listen for the inner voice that comes from God.

CHAPTER SIX

INTROVERTED INTUITION:

*The Illuminating
Spiritual Path*

**Introverted Intuitive Spirituality
INTJ, INFJ**

*Seeking answers to life's mysteries.
Studying the unknown.
Exploring the unseen through the imagination and the intellect.*

As homework for a class on prayer, the instructor told the group, "Each morning this week, set your alarm clock five minutes earlier. Use those five minutes to meditate on the words, 'I belong to God.' Repeat them quietly or envision them in your mind."

The next week, several recipients reported back, "That was so meaningful." "I felt I was awakening into God's care." "It was such a great start to the day that I began setting the alarm *ten* minutes earlier."

An Introverted Intuitive type stared at the group in disbelief. "I gave up after the first morning. My mind kept wandering as different thoughts popped in. 'What does it mean to belong to God? . . . My dog belongs to me. . . . I used to belong to Girl Scouts. . . . I belong getting more sleep. . . .' I couldn't stay with the phrase for more than thirty seconds!"

Introverted Intuitive spirituality seldom follows a pattern, especially if that pattern is prescribed by something outside of the person. Their paths reflect a desire to learn, know, and work out their own spiritual philosophy. Often they are most interested in exploring big questions significant to their worldview and working out their own answers, studying in depth until they reach a solid understanding.

Environments that encourage contemplation and thoughtfulness can provide Introverted Intuitive types with sudden, moving insights into the workings of the universe. They can become frustrated when others seem comfortable with a more superficial understanding of life's mysteries.

> *If I let my mind go, I come up with new ideas about our universe and our Creator. I can't put into words how I know, nor can I provide detailed proof, but when I act on these precognitions, the results prove their accuracy.*
> —Lindsay, 44, consultant

For Introverted Intuitive types, a likely path for soulwork is actively dialoguing with God about prospects for the future. They tend to be systems thinkers by nature, seemingly clairvoyant about what might come to pass, comfortable with the unknown and with the exploration of possibilities. Often, solitude is important to them for this purpose.

> *Once a year I get a combined birthday and anniversary gift—an entire week to be alone at a small retreat center. Each person stays in a private cabin. Throughout the week we can meet with a spiritual director or simply walk the grounds to renew our minds. The first year, I felt guilty about spending so much time away from the family, but now I know that all of us benefit from the rejuvenating experience that week is for me.*
> —Anya, 41, nonprofit manager

Whereas others seek proof, Introverted Intuitive types often experience their most spiritual moments in flashes of intuition—a sense of suddenly knowing something is true for them, perceiving clearly a path they should follow or a plan they should make.

When I was a teenager, my friends thought I was religious just because I was a bit more serious than they were, occasionally thinking about the meaning of life. However, when teachers at our Catholic high school suggested that I consider becoming a priest, I shook my head. I had too many other interests.

Then one day a group of my friends were joking about life as a priest. I pointed out a few positive aspects of that path. Two hours after that "chance" discussion, I applied to seminary. In thirty years I have never regretted my choice of being a priest!

I know now that was an intuitive flash: the priesthood is right for me. These insights are how I experience things authentically. Later, I study to validate what I know to be true. Images and ideas are often a better source of understanding and proof than the most concrete knowledge I can discover.
—Paul, 51, priest

Spirituality becomes a framework through which Introverted Intuitive types can make decisions about every aspect of their lives. They hope to gain wisdom from their Creator to carry themselves through situations with integrity.

I spent an extended period of my life (about fourteen years) questioning the existence of God. What other people told me didn't really matter—I needed to build my own arguments. I came to a more complete understanding of what and who God is, as well as what and who God is not.
—Tim, 52, attorney

Prayer

As in the above "I belong to God" story, prayer for Introverted Intuitive types is seldom a straightforward undertaking. Their inner worlds are so busy that one thought often brings connections to a dozen others, sidetracking whatever it was they were praying about. They do best through methods that engage (or harness) the imagination.

- Introverted Intuitive types might set aside time for writing, such as journaling, to capture prayer requests or thoughts, hopes, and aspirations. They may also write out their prayers as a way of staying focused.

Often, I read a passage of Scripture and then journal about what it means to me. What questions do I have? How does it apply to me? To those I know? It makes me slow down and absorb the words instead of only grasping the big ideas.
　　—Mark, 19, university student

- Prayer techniques that engage the imagination may also prove fruitful, such as imagining one's self as part of a Bible story and recording any insights that come. Other techniques include writing imagined conversations or poetry to express their thoughts or access their insights.
- They may also engage in reflection or meditation, often combining these times with forms of study so that new thoughts and information can feed their prayers.
- Some Introverted Intuitive types purposefully add structure by keeping prayer journals in which they write down specific praises, prayer requests, and ongoing concerns for friends, relatives, or problems in the world. Others find it helpful to combine prayer with solitary walks or other forms of exercise. While their mind often wanders, by trying to pray with some sort of order, they can pull their thoughts back to the next prayer concern when they realize they are off track.

For years I thought that I was "bad" at prayer. My mind always wandered and I felt guilty about it, even though prayer time often fed, illuminated, delighted, and comforted me. Now I understand that my Intuition was at work, connecting one thought with another and providing new insights. Instead of condemning myself, I bought a notebook to list the things I want to be consistent about in prayer. Now I can choose to flit or focus!
　　—Esther, 48, photographer

Worship

Whether worshiping in a crowd or a small group, Introverted Intuitive types look for atmospheres that enrich their knowledge and allow their souls room to chart their own reactions or interpretations. If things become too familiar or rote, they easily fall into thinking about other things even as they repeat prayers or join in singing.

- Variety is key to Introverted Intuitive worship. They are better able to pay attention to services, prayers, or rituals when they are fresh and unfamiliar. They may also enjoy helping to plan such services.

The church my family attended when I was growing up let the teens plan one service each month. We wrote the prayers, chose the hymns or other music, came up with skits, changed the decorations, and even sometimes shared in giving the sermon. Looking back, it was the perfect environment for me—constant variety and a clear message that our ideas about faith and God were valued.
—Alyssa, 36, writer

- Introverted Intuitive types tend not to share feelings or emotions readily and are usually more comfortable in worship settings where people stay rather calm.

Sometimes I feel like worship actually interrupts my worship—unless I've consciously chosen to attend a service filled with movement and hand-clapping, the more other people wave their arms, the more I feel like sitting still!
—Dan, 52, psychologist

- They also enjoy a certain organization or structure to oral talks or sermons, making them easier to follow. Otherwise, their minds may wander off from the information being presented to make their own connections so that they miss the rest of the message. To compensate, some Introverted Intuitive types take short notes rather than lose focus altogether.

Study

The inner world of the mind is where Introverted Intuition flourishes. Various forms of study are often their most meaningful spiritual paths. They might return to school for formal classes or education, being naturally motivated to learn more about areas of interest to them.

- While Introverted Intuitive types enjoy listening to qualified experts or participating in discussions, if they need answers to a particular question, they are likely to go to a library or bookstore, read several sources, then come to their own conclusions. They also enjoy in-depth study of a variety of topics, retreating with a stack of books to an inspiring place to indulge in the luxury of spending time with intellectual explorations that feed the soul.

- Introverted Intuitive types often pursue study for the purpose of designing or planning educational materials or presentations that will help others deepen their beliefs.

Once while teaching teen religious education classes, I spent hours reading different interpretations of the Bible passage we were studying. I then wrote a play for the students to perform, quite sure that would be the best way for them to grasp the rich symbolism of the passage. Their performance was enthusiastic and the ensuing discussion rewarding for me. One of the boys remarked, "I can't believe you put so much time into writing this just for us." I explained how much fun—and meaningful—the process was to me!
—Tessa, 28, financial planner

- They may also spearhead or assist with projects that require in-depth research. One Introverted Intuitive person rewrote the traditional liturgies of her church to make them more applicable to modern-day circumstances, finding it one of the most meaningful avenues to soulwork she had experienced.

Service

Introverted Intuitive types may see so palpably how the world could be a better place that their best avenues of service are often attempts to bring those visions to reality.

- Introverted Intuitive types might help others find innovative solutions to problems. Coming up with the right focus on an issue or the best way to assist others often fosters their own deep spirituality as they use their talents in this way.
- Introverted Intuitive types often join in planning or leadership endeavors to influence others through the power of their ideas. They enjoy putting their ingenuity to work on efforts of spiritual significance, using their insightful, scholarly perspectives.

I never really thought of myself as a leader, but I joined the advisory team for our women's ministry. I soon discovered that my perspective was quite different from everyone else's, and quite helpful, according

to the group. Now I more readily look for task forces where my ideas are needed—especially when something needs to change.
  —Anne, 36, homemaker

- Introverted Intuitive types may also use writing or teaching to express their spirituality, helping people clarify what they believe. Drawing on their own insights and wealth of knowledge, they can be inspiring teachers, especially with those who engage in the process at a similar intellectual level.

Other Forms of Soulwork

With their ability to make connections, Introverted Intuitive types can glean spiritual insights from a variety of pursuits. They constantly look to develop and deepen their insights.

- Artistic endeavors or contemplating the work of others is often enriching soulwork. Many Introverted Intuitive types who play musical instruments, paint, or sculpt lose track of time as they do so. These pastimes allow for reflection on themes of spirituality, relationships, wholeness, or hope.
- Engaging actively in debate or dialogue with knowledgeable people about possibilities for society and the best ways to match current knowledge with new, more effective direction offers Introverted Intuitives another avenue for soulwork. They may serve on task forces where they can influence ideas and make things happen.

I often interpret my ideas, insights, and perceptions as spiritual messages that are meant to guide me or at least be taken into consideration. I don't tell others about my feeling of being "chosen" by God, but it radically changed my thinking. I sometimes sense a prophetic calling—trying to bring spirituality and God-centered principles to the ills that face our modern world.
  —Aubrey, 55, writer

- Reading widely; finding insights in scientific, secular, fictional, and religious writings comprises soulwork for Introverted Intuitives.

In short, Introverted Intuitive spirituality helps all of us remember that

- delving into the depth of spiritual knowledge adds insights to life,
- imagination can help us tap into the mysteries of God,
- the mind and spirit can work together for soulwork,
- thinking about what *could be* can change the world.

The Second Half of Life's Spiritual Journey

While Introverted Intuition is about pondering life's mysteries and developing ideas that allow for human growth, eventually life grows short. Or, as do all personalities, the Introverted Intuitive types begin to wonder whether they have found sufficient meaning and purpose. If they continue on their current path, what will they miss?

Often at this stage, the Introverted Intuitive types have developed their natural spiritual path. Then, richness comes through using their inferior function, Extraverted Sensing. This involves

- experiencing the sacred in what is immediate and real, not in possibilities and the ideal;
- finding support for one's spiritual path or evidence of the Creator in the details of creation, such as the beauty of rock crystals or the birth of a child;
- applying spiritual teachings to daily, practical purposes;
- enjoying the straightforward gift of being alive.

While Introverted Intuitive types may continue many of their favorite methods of soulwork, here are some examples of what they found as they journeyed on into Extraverted Sensing:

> *I have a sense of being in the right place at the right time doing the immediate thing that most needs doing for another person. The simple act of reaching out brings meaning and purpose to my actions.*

> *In one of our last conversations before my mother died, she and I took turns naming our favorite food, song, lake, and so on. I'd never really bothered with those little things before. Now I understand the true gift of knowing those specifics about my mother. I feel a special connection with Mom every time I eat scones with boysenberry jam because she loved them so!*

I used to ignore traditional liturgies and rote prayers. How could they have meaning when one could say them without thinking about the words? Lately, though, I find a certain comfort in reciting centuries-old litanies. Some are so complete, capturing in a few lines what it has taken me years to express to God. A few years ago, news of the space shuttle explosion came as I taught a class on spirituality. After informing the group, I turned to the Book of Common Prayer and used its timeless prayer for the dead to lead the group. Afterward, several participants mentioned that they planned to find a copy, now that they knew the richness it contained.

Recently I realized that I had never really looked at a single flower before. I'd focus on the overall effect of a bouquet or a garden, not realizing the intricate design of each individual blossom with its stamen, petals, and filaments. Now at least once a day I try to find God in life's details.

I'm spending far more of my time exploring the world by actually going on (instead of just planning for others) an international loaned-executive program. I want to see how the strategies I developed from afar turn out in practical terms. I now enjoy working beside others as we dig wells and I teach new irrigation techniques. Experiencing as well as envisioning being the hands of God for others brings new meaning to my soul.

Any of the Sensing pathways (chapters 3 and 4) can bring this kind of rest and richness to Introverted Intuitive types when they allow their dominant function a time of rest and let the Spirit guide their thoughts and actions.

INTJ

Introversion Intuition
Thinking Judging

Spirituality in the inner world of ideas and insights

I devoted myself to study and to explore by wisdom all that is done under heaven.
—*Ecclesiastes 1:13*

Greatest Gifts

Creating visions of the future; Using reason and objectivity to design methods, strategies, and structures for conceptual understanding; Building paradigms based on intellectual acumen

Role in Community

Challenging traditions, breaking new ground, and questioning the status quo; Adding an independent outlook in their endeavors to fashion a better world

---

INTJs tend to be strong individualists who seek novel, logical ways to look at the world. They are visionaries who work hard to attain big-picture goals. With their clear sense of direction, they are tireless and determined in developing hypotheses, ideas, and principles. They see how all the parts fit together, creating new models.

Using their dominant function, Introverted Intuition, is the natural starting place for soulwork. However, their auxiliary or second function,

Extraverted Thinking, calls them to find some sort of community, be it a small group or a formal religious organization, for further exploration of spiritual truths.

Soulwork through the Second Function

INTJs tend to seek out settings where others are also on a rigorous search for spiritual insights, clarity, and flaws and incongruities. INTJs might look for a spiritual community that emphasizes adult education so they can find others at a similar intellectual level. This allows them to be open about their spirituality and receive input from others while exploring or determining truths.

> *I used to be pretty adept at "doing my will in God's name"—I'd envision the entire solution to a problem and expect other people to implement it without a whole lot of debate. Now I try to get their input while I'm still in process. This is never easy, but I don't feel a need to control the whole operation anymore.*
> —Nathan, 56, minister

INTJs might also use their Extraverted Thinking function in asking a wise, competent person whom they trust to listen to them with a logical or problem-solving mindset to identify issues and prioritize them.

Within these settings, INTJs might seek to use Extraverted Thinking by engaging in any of the exercises listed for the Thinking preference (pages 145-149), with goals such as

- receiving input from others while exploring or determining spiritual truths,
- organizing and evaluating their insights,
- reaching conclusions by evaluating the pros and cons of different alternatives,
- realigning their inner convictions,
- working with others to conquer life's problems.

All of these might help them bring clarity to their beliefs and breadth to their soulwork.

> *I don't naturally seek others out, but now I have a mentor whose brilliance I truly admire and respect. He lets me talk, think, analyze, and express myself, then asks a few cogent questions, which gets me through all the muddle and back on track.*
> —Jackie, 45, small business owner

What Might Push INTJs Away from Their Spiritual Path

With their rigorous quest for truth, INTJs often find themselves in religious settings contrary to their preferred soulwork. Common themes we heard from INTJs we interviewed included

- preferring to work out their beliefs by themselves or with a trusted other. Many INTJs find it hard to accept a preestablished system or conventional model of spirituality.

  I sometimes joke that I'm on a lifelong quest for the ultimate, integrated theory of what it is to be human—who we are, how we're made, and how we ought to relate to each other and the world. My personal spiritual experience makes it necessary to include God in the picture, but I can't see our spiritual lives as separate from, nor opposed to, our physical existence.
  —Kay, 55, university professor

- being at odds with the idea of a higher power. Some INTJs find the concept of God difficult, especially if their conceptualization is one of an aloof and imperious God who controls or punishes people. In this context, some INTJs may view spirituality as a crutch for the timid and fearful.

- developing deep but narrow interests, many of which are more pressing than spirituality and respond better to logical thinking. The spiritual aspects of INTJs' lives may be ignored, overlooked, or postponed. INTJs may prefer to stay neutral on the topic until they find the motivation or make the time to give soulwork their *own* deep scrutiny.

- feeling reluctance to share their innermost selves with others. Some INTJs regret not being able to share their interpretation of God even with their own children, instead leaving them to come to their own conclusions. Privacy and reserve characterize some INTJs, especially in personal matters.

  What I regret as an INTJ is that, whatever my personal perception and interpretation of God, it is a very private matter. I find it difficult to share with others, even my children, and I realize that they are left to come to their own conclusions.
  —Jason, 35, financial analyst

Trusted spiritual advisors, friends, and family can help INTJs find an enriching spiritual path by

- being willing to admit their own doubts and intellectually explore the possible truths of our faith;
- accepting that a cognitive approach to spirituality is valid;
- sharing stories of how they found guidance from God;
- asking about INTJs' ideas and dreams for the future, listening, and granting them independence of thought and approach.

When Life Is Difficult

The fourth, or *inferior*, function for INTJs is Extraverted Sensing. With their emphasis on insights and new ideas, tapping into the Extraverted Sensing realm of what is happening right now is a struggle. In times of stress, the inferior function can erupt, changing the INTJ's behavior into a caricature of ESFPs and ESTPs for whom it is the *dominant* function.

For INTJs, the following circumstances might trigger the inferior function in times of stress:

- When they have to work with too many details that do not fall into logical frameworks. This situation may cause INTJs to feel out of control or to become too detail-bound.
- When unexpected events derail their appropriate and carefully perfected strategies.

I had worked so carefully to ensure that we had tended to every aspect in the age discrimination suit our company faced. We had concrete proof that the person we had laid off had not performed well for several years and there was no pattern of similar firings. Our case went out the window when the person who had filed the suit died of a sudden stroke. Being right no longer mattered, but the chaos that followed his death went on for months.
   —Vern, 61, operations officer

- When they are forced to "extravert" too much. Without alone time to reenergize, INTJs can quickly become bogged down. They may feel so pulled to accomplish things in a crisis that they have no time to consider the best course of action or the impact they are having on others.
- When they can't adjust their internal models of the situation. INTJs can lose their objectivity either by being so distracted by

the outer world that they have no time to reconsider their plans or by isolating themselves so much that they are closed to new information.

Often, the worst times for INTJs are when they understand their predicament, account for all of its contingencies, carefully make and follow their plan, and still achieve less than adequate results or responses. Perhaps they overused their dominant Intuition function by relying on their own abilities to generate possibilities, control the circumstances, and calm the storm.

> *I was cultivating my business when two merger opportunities came along. They both were aligned with my own very successful enterprise. I went after these two new possibilities with gusto. I became so one-sided that I was a classic candidate for burnout. Other than in my professional roles, I was like a robot. Life then lost its spark—I realized that to keep control in the turbulent international market place, I had delegated everything but my work. Almost too late, I discovered that I was missing life! God waited for me to understand my one-sidedness and to open up to the needs of those around me, not just the clients I had served so successfully through my work.*
> —James, 33, architect

In these situations, INTJs might become uncharacteristically hostile, avoiding or denying reality by watching too much television, playing computer games, exercising too frequently, or overeating. They may also obsess about unimportant details. When these symptoms appear, a totally different approach to soulwork often helps. INTJs might *purposefully* pursue Extraverted Sensing. Its *conscious use* requires INTJs to shut down what is usually easiest—Introverted Intuition—which may have gotten out of control. By doing so, INTJs can get out into the world, opening up new sources of information and ideas.

Ways to consciously engage the Sensing function include

- engaging in detailed crafts or other projects where following directions is essential. Some INTJs choose needlework, gardening, woodworking, and the like.
- reducing the crisis to the facts—its most basic, elemental, and straightforward needs, then moving forward with efficient action.
- pursuing physical activities such as running, biking, energetic volleyball games, or other sports. Being with people and being

a bit wild and crazy can free the soul and provide fresh inspirations.

In the chosen activity, the key is setting aside one's hunches and inner possibilities and using reality to adjust one's thinking. One INTJ expressed, "God waited for me to understand my one-sidedness and to open up to the *immediate* needs of those around me instead of only concentrating on future plans for them."

As an INTJ, I am thankful for
>   my keen insights and inspirations;
>   my love of challenge and complex problems requiring elegant approaches;
>   my ease with systems, strategies, and structures;
>   my determination and drive to perfect my ideas.

When life is difficult I can find support by
>   developing a plan, then loosening control and accepting the outcome;
>   inviting logical feedback from a respected and trusted colleague;
>   giving myself ample time for play and rejuvenation.

To honor myself and my pathway to God, I can
>   satisfy my intellect with prayer, study, or retreat;
>   observe the little things right now—the momentary pleasures that can enrich my life when I take time to notice;
>   put my mind to work for greater purposes that serve my spiritual philosophy.

INFJ

Introversion Intuition Feeling Judging

Spirituality in the inner world of ideas and possibilities

Therefore encourage one another and build each other up, just as in fact you are doing.
—*1 Thessalonians 5:11*

Greatest Gifts

Seeing life, people, relationships, or the potential of others in a discerning fashion; Envisioning innovative solutions to problems

Role in Community

Contributing future-oriented ideas; Understanding the feelings and motivations of others; Finding creative ways for people to accomplish tasks while making the process enjoyable

---

INFJs often have creative and independent ideas for dealing with complex issues and are adept at getting systems to work for people. They tend to focus on long-term possibilities for humankind. INFJs seek life paths that allow them to mirror their integrity, build on their inner ideals, and use their inspirations for the common good. Others can count on them to follow through.

Using their dominant function, Introverted Intuition, is the natural starting place for soulwork. However, their auxiliary or second function,

Extraverted Feeling, calls them to join with others, whether in small groups or in a larger faith community.

Soulwork through the Second Function

Many INFJs are hesitant to share their spiritual journey with people other than close friends or in one-on-one situations. However, they enjoy meaningful group discussions. Further, talking through ideas with others helps them tap into their personal feelings about issues and circumstances rather than focus only on possibilities.

> *I choose my study companions and experiences carefully. I get frustrated by pat answers or any format that doesn't allow me to put forth my own conclusions or add to what the leader or materials are saying. I'd rather take the text to a quiet spot and try to figure out what it means to me and my own circumstances. However, being in a group inspires me in a way solitude can't provide. That's worth my time even if I don't necessarily learn anything new.*
> —Peri, 36, editor

Talking through experiences with others helps INFJs understand how an event or idea has affected them. They may not want advice, but an empathetic listening ear often helps them clarify values or consider the viewpoints of others.

> *I felt like there was a wall between me and my coworkers, as if my presence and problems didn't even show a blip on their radar screens. After obsessing with the matter too long, I finally talked with a person I could trust who just listened as I poured out my feelings. As I described my dilemma, I gained relief from my pent-up emotions and could see a way out of the situation.*
> —Corinne, 27, administrator

With the people they choose, INFJs might seek to use Extraverted Feeling by engaging in any of the exercises listed for the Feeling function (pages 193-198), with goals such as

- gaining input from others to understand diverse viewpoints,
- engaging in meaningful discussions that help them mold their own beliefs,
- helping create new programs or opportunities,

- encouraging and inspiring each other to reach their full potential,
- perhaps taking a leadership role in forming or leading a small group for study or other soulwork.

All of these might help them bring clarity to their beliefs and breadth to their soulwork.

What Might Push INFJs Away from Their Spiritual Path

If INFJs are somehow blocked from their unique, Intuitive spiritual path or not affirmed in their strengths, they may lose their natural affinity for the unseen. Common themes we heard from the people we interviewed included

- being in disharmonious circumstances. INFJs tend to idealize people and situations. They want everyone around them to honor commitments, strive to get along, appreciate individual contributions, and help the outsider. If they cannot find a spiritual community that is as committed and mature as they can envision, they may choose to stay away.
- lack of variety in spiritual rituals, prayers, or practices. INFJs tend to prefer taking part in new litanies and a variety of soulwork. Otherwise, their minds often wander as they repeat the familiar words or ceremonies.
- being in atmospheres that do not allow for examination of beliefs. While INFJs may intuitively connect with soulwork, many also need to go through a deep process of questioning and study to validate a belief and value system. Soulwork without this process may lack meaning for them.
- having frustrations with their own lack of perfection. INFJs often fall short of their own expectations for pursuing spirituality, for being actively and directly involved with others, or for sharing their ideas for improving programs or projects. In addition, INFJs are often hesitant to speak up, even when they clearly see solutions to problems that would aid others. They don't want to "toot their own horns" to be appreciated for the expertise they can contribute.

Trusted spiritual advisors, friends, and family can help INFJs find an enriching spiritual path by

- understanding that they are independent and original people who often have the need to "go it alone" in matters of faith,

- meeting in a small group in a disciplined way to encourage each other's spiritual growth,
- sharing how they have deepened their faith so they have more to give to others,
- allowing them the freedom to strive for what they envision and lending support while they do so, saying, "Go for it, you can do it!"

After many years of trying to pray "perfectly," it suddenly occurred to me that I had never prayed "well." My ideal was shattered, but bit by bit I came to understand that, while I hadn't met the ideal described in books, my prayer style was all right with God. I quit trying to follow pathways others had prescribed for me. I know now that many people of my type dislike formula, regular or repetitive prayers. My style is spiritual and my own prayers work best for me.
—Evelyn, 56, counselor

When Life Is Difficult

The fourth, or *inferior,* function for INFJs is Extraverted Sensing. With their emphasis on the insights and new ideas, tapping into the Extraverted Sensing realm of what is happening right now is a struggle. In times of stress, their inferior function can erupt, changing the INFJ's behavior into a caricature of ESTPs and ESFPs for whom it is the *dominant* function.

For INFJs, the following circumstances might trigger the inferior function in times of stress:
- When their natural tendency toward perfection is triggered. INFJs may deepen their own sense of loss by holding themselves accountable for things beyond their control. When others are involved, INFJs may berate themselves for not being supportive enough, not finding the right things to say or do, or not owning up to their own part in failures.
- When they are forced to monitor too many details, a task that requires them to use their inferior function, Extraverted Sensing. They may overlook crucial facts (typically a weakness) or spend too much time on unimportant items.
- When other people are too full of doom and gloom, dragging the INFJ down along with them.

- When they are expected to "extravert" too much. If INFJs spend too much of their time in the company of others, they may find themselves exhausted.

  The week of my 72-year-old father's wedding was difficult. Every minute was booked with appointments, chauffeuring, and family responsibilities. Friday evening found me on the couch with my third bowl of popcorn, unable to rise or contemplate greeting another relative or friend.
  —Bob, 55, teacher

Often, the worst times for INFJs are when they realize that no matter how hard they try to come up with a solution, the problem is beyond their influence or command. They may have overused their dominant Intuition function by envisioning too many possibilities, trying to resolve things alone, researching information, and pursuing their more solitary spiritual path. They often then further isolate themselves, convinced that the whole world is against them.

  When my illness was diagnosed, I thought I could handle my own needs. After all, I had studied meditation, I knew which spiritual readings would comfort me, and I took the time to do these things. The results? Nothing. I was still as frightened as before. I felt as if my carefully crafted soulwork was a failure. This was also the point at which my true healing began, because I finally shared with my spouse my fears about the choices I was facing. I learned that in despair help can come to me through other people. My own resources can only go so far.
  —Jackie, 45, industrial psychologist

In these situations, INFJs might display unnatural pessimism. They may also overindulge in television or exercise, eat way too much or way too little, head out on mindless shopping trips or other purposeless activities, finding little joy in them. When these symptoms appear, a totally different approach to soulwork often helps. INFJs might *purposefully* pursue Extraverted Sensing. Its *conscious use* requires INFJs to shut down what is usually easiest—Introverted Intuition—which may have gotten out of control. In doing so INFJs again engage with other people or outside activities to broaden their perspective.

Ways to consciously engage the Sensing function include

- giving full attention to pursuits where following plans or directions to the letter may be necessary. Examples are wallpapering, painting, jigsaw puzzles, and intricate craft projects such as needlepoint or electronics kits.
- engaging in physical pursuits such as biking, aerobics, or swimming, where the emphasis is on body movements, speed, techniques, and awareness of the here and now.
- concentrating on the facts of a situation—what was actually said, what really happened. Ignoring the implications and possible outcomes for a bit allows their Intuition to rest. The same rest can come through time spent in natural surroundings.

In the chosen activity, the key is to shut down thoughts of the future or the dilemma they face and concentrate on what is good about the present moment, the world around them, and life in general. As one INFJ put it, "When I admitted that I couldn't handle everything by myself, my true healing began. Once I shared my fears, I learned how others could help me."

As an INFJ, I am thankful for
my creativity that allows me to envision different solutions,
my optimism in trying circumstances,
my ability to help people recognize their potential,
the way I can communicate to others.

When life is difficult, I can find support by
realizing that it is okay to seek help,
finding a listening ear so that I can discern my feelings,
assessing the details and tasks, giving away what I cannot handle.

To honor myself and my pathway to God, I can
find creative ways to engage my imagination;
create space for myself to be alone with my thoughts, prayers, or musings;
notice the spiritual in the details of creation.

PART THREE

THINKING AND FEELING SPIRITUALITY

INTRODUCTION:
THE SUNFLOWER EXERCISE

Before you read further, try the following soulwork exercise, based on *The Sunflower: On the Possibilities and Limits of Forgiveness* by Simon Wiesenthal[1] As best you can, imagine yourself in Wiesenthal's shoes:

You are a Jewish prisoner in a German concentration camp. A nurse demands that you accompany her to the hospital room of a dying Nazi soldier. The Nazi soldier tells you of the idealism instilled in him by the Hitler Youth, his days as a soldier, and finally the atrocities he committed as his unit cleared one of the ghettos in Russia. "I am left here with my guilt. In the last hours of my life you are with me. I do not know who you are. I only know that you are a Jew and that is enough . . . I have longed to talk about it to a Jew and beg forgiveness from him." He asks for your forgiveness.

Your own mother had been dragged from a ghetto just weeks before in a Nazi raid. What would you do?

Wiesenthal listened to the soldier's confession, then turned and walked out of the room without saying a word. What would you have done? Why? Consider whether or not Wiesenthal should have forgiven the soldier. Make two lists: reasons to forgive and reasons not to forgive.

To discuss Wiesenthal's dilemma at one retreat, we formed groups of Thinking types and Feeling types. Each group made lists of reasons to forgive and reasons not to forgive and reported back to everyone.

The Thinking group began their report with the issue of "should."

- What *should* he do? How could any of us decide what Wiesenthal should have done?
- Our discussion highlighted the schism between a corporal and an individual sense of guilt and forgiveness.

When it comes to spiritual issues, those with Thinking preferences have a desire to define what they know to be true, to wrestle with universal principles such as justice and truth, to debate and inquire and dialogue about practices and beliefs. That's where the Thinking group's discussions about *The Sunflower* exercise started.

The Feeling group started right in with what they would have done and why, coming to terms with their own values about the role of forgiveness. Their list started with truly putting themselves in Wiesenthal's shoes:

- We would like to believe we could forgive, offer compassion, but know that instead we might attack, "You're getting what you deserve . . ."
- How could someone let go of the anger and even feel as if they had forgiven?

Those with Feeling preferences want to consider the impact of practices on people and find personal meaning. That is where their discussion started.

Yet once the groups finished their definitions of words and values and principles, their lists of pros and cons were very similar. As you review the following themes, consider which nuances resonate more with you.

The Power of Forgiveness

Thinkers said, "Hatred harms the person who harbors it. It perpetuates wrongs, fixates on negativity, and blocks us from going on toward wholeness." Feelers said, "Forgiveness frees, allows for compassion, lets us move on."

The Process of Forgiveness

Thinkers said, "One could forgive later if not in the moment, for the sake of mental health. One might not have the capacity at the time." Feelers said, "It was abusive for the soldier to ask for forgiveness so suddenly. Forgiveness is a process."

The Place of Forgiveness

Thinkers said, "Who can bestow forgiveness? Should the Jewish community be involved? The crimes against Wiesenthal and his family were committed by other soldiers, not this one, so how can he speak for the others? And isn't forgiveness God's to bestow?" Feelers said, "What was the intent behind the soldier's request? Only God can judge the heart and whether granting forgiveness might actually just foster the soldier's self-centeredness and insincerity."

Yes, the words and vocabulary of the groups were different, as was the order in which these topics were discussed. However, as the groups talked about their responses, we had an overwhelming sense that when Thinkers and Feelers are given ample time to discuss a topic, they cover a significant amount of overlapping ground. Further, we experienced a phenomenally rich discussion of a profound moral question when both sides were allowed to follow their paths of inquiry without being interrupted or judged by the other. We all left the retreat with a deep understanding of the issues involved.

The Paths of Thinking Spirituality

Have confidence in the truth, although you may not be able to comprehend it, although you may suppose its sweetness to be bitter, although you
may shrink from it at first. Trust in the Truth . . . Have faith in the Truth
and live it.[1]

—*Buddha,* Dhammapada

Thinking types find satisfying soulwork through

- living the spiritual life through the intellect;
- gaining spiritual insights by observation, study, or debate;
- appreciating the beauty of wisdom and the clarity of teachings;
- seeing applications for standards of accountability and structures for fairness and order;
- learning through exploration of the "thorny" questions of life;
- working to establish universal principles and truths;
- evaluating the logic, effectiveness, and justice of spiritual practices or beliefs.

Preferred Extraverted Thinking Soulwork (Ch. 7: ESTJ and ENTJ)	Preferred Introverted Thinking Soulwork (Ch. 8: ISTP and INTP)
• Prayer or meditation as a search for answers, truths, guiding principles, and explanations	• Prayer or meditation by dialoguing with God about principles and ethics
• Soulwork through debate and discourse	• Soulwork through integrating observations and rational thought
• Active spiritual life, in the midst of duty and a quest for effectiveness	• Reflective spiritual life, in the course of inquiry, study, and wrestling with difficult issues
• Service through working to change structures that seem ineffective, corrupt, or unfair	• Service through determining systems for actualization of improvements

Suggestions for Thinking Spirituality

1. Consider the fruits of the Spirit: love, joy, peace, patience, kindness, goodness, faithfulness, gentleness, and self-control. Simi-
   larly, in the Buddhist tradition, the ten perfections are generosity,
   virtue, doing without, wisdom, energy, forbearance, truthfulness,

resolution, love, and serenity. Choose one of these fruits or perfections and answer the following questions:

- How would you define it?
- What happens when it guides your life?
- What happens when you fail to have it guide your life?
- If you were to make changes in your life to reflect this fruit or this perfection, what would they be?
- What would be the outcomes or results?

2. Kahlil Gibran said, "I have learned silence from the talkative, toleration from the intolerant, and kindness from the unkind; yet strange, I am ungrateful to those teachers."[2]

- What are the paradoxes in the above quote?
- When have you found these paradoxes to be true?
- What were the costs and benefits of learning in this fashion?
- Record some examples in your life where the statement has been true or false. What and who were your teachers?
- In what other areas in your life could you use a "teacher"?

3. As you read or hear about a topic, gather the facts and meanings. Devote the majority of your study time to discerning the correctness of what you have read. Is it true? Even if it's true, is it right or wrong? Positive or negative? Then, consider the impact of your deliberations on yourself or others.

4. For the discipline of simplicity: Simone Weil said, "The danger is not lest the soul should doubt whether there is any bread, but lest, by a lie, it should persuade itself that it is not hungry."[3] How could your need for clarity and truth block you from trying any of the "simple" forms of soulwork? Your need to be competent or right?

5. For the discipline of celebration: Find your own way to acknowledge those times when justice prevails, truths are made clear, or reason and logic result in an elegant solution or outcome. Some examples to stimulate your thoughts of celebration include: Reward your colleagues when they pull their own weight. Do something special with your child when he or she holds to a principle. Revel in the concise and logical writing of a favorite author. Set aside time to appreciate the technique and splendor of Bach organ cantatas. Take time to laugh hard at the cleverness of comedy or the absurdities of fools. Covenant with God about

a change in your soulwork or guiding principles and mark each successful anniversary (perhaps weekly at first) of the keeping of that covenant.

6. Find two or three people who share your willingness to include objective analysis or doubt as part of soulwork. Meet regularly to discuss a sacred text, a secular book, or a current issue. Begin by pointing out everything that is *wrong* with the opinions presented by the authors or text and then move toward finding those aspects with which you can agree.

7. To bring rest to the work of the mind, consider something that simply *cannot* be explained logically by what is currently known: the vastness of the night skies, the infinite varieties of bird species, or the precise balance of elements that makes life on Earth possible. Observe the power of a thunderstorm or the crashing of the ocean's pounding surf. Watch a butterfly come out of its cocoon. Set out honey for ants and wait for the army to communicate the feast. Ponder the infiniteness and boundaries of your intellectual ability to understand the world.

8. Take a risk. Venture into an area of spirituality where you have no previous experience and are therefore not an expert. For example: Study the role of liturgical dance in worship (you don't have to actually *dance*), offer to teach children in your spiritual community, or take a course in counseling or other matters of the heart. Sometimes by opening yourself to areas where you have no established competency, you can relinquish a possibly tight rein of control.

9. Set aside time to listen to music that frees your mind from analysis— instrumentals or songs with words in a language you don't speak. Perhaps record several of these on a single tape so that you can have uninterrupted music for soulwork while relaxing in a sacred spot.

10. Reconsider your spiritual life through the lens of truth. Strive for honesty as you pray about your hopes, fears, doubts, and blessings. Perhaps use the moral codes of your faith (Ten Commandments, Golden Rule, or Five Precepts) to reexamine whether your actions are guided by your principles. Where might change need to occur?

Extraverted Thinking Soulwork

1. George Fox, founder of the Religious Society of Friends (Quakers), implored us to "Do rightly, justly, truly, holily, equally to all people in all things; and that is according to that of God in everyone, and the witness of God, and the wisdom of God, and the life of God in yourselves."[4] Try each day to perform one act that restores justice, applies fairness, or does right by another. Perhaps it is as simple as instructing your children that whoever cuts the pie chooses his or her slice last, bringing to management's attention a policy that is unfair, or finding an opportunity to return a favor or kind deed.

2. For the discipline of study: Indulge in the study of a scientific subject or aspect of natural history that interests you—either through reading or by direct observation. What principles are in operation? What explanations can you discover? Discuss your ideas with others. How might these principles and explanations help you understand your own experiences and the choices you face? What might be put into action?

3. For the discipline of prayer: Consider a single precept or dogma of your spiritual tradition. Meditate or pray about the implications of following or not following it and your rationale for your choice.

4. Prayer from Kenya:

   From the cowardice that dare not face new truth
   From the laziness that is contented with half truth
   From the arrogance that thinks it knows all truth,
   Good Lord, deliver me.[5]

   To what topics could you apply your gift of Thinking? Select an interesting global or personal issue. Examples might be urban sprawl, societal responsibility toward education, allocation of resources, or something within your own sphere of influence. Evaluate the causes and effects of the situation and the pros and cons of different approaches or solutions. How have truths that were honored in the past been violated? As you ponder the issue, how are you called to work toward an answer?

Introverted Thinking Soulwork

1. Choose a spiritual concept such as truth, love, wholeness, joy, justice, or fairness.
   - What are its attributes?
   - How can you tell when it exists?
   - How does this concept work effectively with people, organizations, or the world? Ineffectively?

Ponder this information as tangible evidence of these intangible forces. How does your understanding of these concepts deepen?

2. For the discipline of prayer: Consider what you *know* to be true about an aspect of spirituality such as
   - the strength of forgiveness,
   - the power of making peace,
   - the Golden Rule and other spiritual precepts,
   - the Creator or the connectedness of the universe.

Where are the consistencies? How can you use this information to reconcile the inconsistencies with other thoughts you may have? Apply this same process to the platitudes and slogans from the secular world, such as, "Nice folks finish last," in order to find your own truth.

3. For the discipline of study: What major question(s) hinders your soulwork? Evil in the world? The injustices you see? The mythical or unproven aspects of the spiritual tradition in which you were raised? The lack of true compassion in people who claim to be spiritual? Sort through and identify the key source of discord or resistance. Then work through this issue either in discussion with a trusted other who has explained it to his or her own satisfaction, or through reading, or through your own thoughtful meditation.

4. In what situations do you feel inadequate, incompetent, or ill at ease? What seems to be a theme in your complaints? Think about these areas with a critical yet compassionate eye. How could these be areas where you might learn more about the workings of your soul?

CHAPTER SEVEN

EXTRAVERTED THINKING:

The Analytical Spiritual Path

Extraverted Thinking Spirituality
ESTJ, ENTJ

Questioning and critiquing all matter of things spiritual.
Searching for truth and justice.
Connecting soulwork to the logical, analytical, and objective part of us.

A t one *SoulTypes* seminar, participants formed Thinking and Feeling groups to discuss the resources that help them most when life gets difficult. As the groups reported on their discussions, the Extraverted Thinking participants said, "Our discussion was profound. So often others judge us for how we talk about emotional issues, saying we're too cold and analytical. But in this group we *understood* each other. And that's all we'll say because, if we report out, we're quite certain you'll once again view us as cold-hearted!"

Extraverted Thinking spirituality involves seeking truth, working toward justice, and grounding actions in solid beliefs and principles. Rather than take things on faith, Extraverted Thinking types examine evidence or develop logical frameworks for what they believe.

> *After I got married, there were peaks and valleys in my spirituality. Between building a career, a house, and a family, life was very full. However, one day while we were driving home from preschool, my daughter asked, "Why does that building have a t up on top?" I realized then that I would be derelict in my duty if my children did not receive spiritual instruction. I began to analyze my own faith. What did I believe? Just what were the pros and cons of involvement and what system could speak to real issues in a direct and honest way? It took some soul-searching, but I concluded that it was more reasonable to have a faith than not.*
> —Meg, 38, operations manager

That's people with Extraverted Thinking Spirituality—building moral foundations for themselves, their families, and their communities, and widening their social circles and providing logical analysis of traditions and rituals. Their key role in spiritual realms is to challenge standard thinking by creating openings for inquiry into human nature, the origins of all we know, and our reason for being.

For Extraverted Thinking types, their outward, goal-oriented leadership is often motivated by their spirituality. They want to be a part of forces larger than themselves to correct injustices and solve problems.

> *Somewhere during the past years, my faith went from something I did to something that was meaningful. My spirituality provides friends on whom I can count for support, a vehicle to serve others, a sense that I'm a part of something bigger than myself, and a connectedness to others worldwide. Overall, I've concluded that it's logical to believe.*
> —Susan, 48 purchasing agent

Skepticism is a tool for developing new insights or applications of universal truths. Extraverted Thinking types grasp core principles as standards of conduct for themselves and others. Formed through analysis, pragmatism, and skepticism, their beliefs can run deep. Their most spiritual moments often come when they are allowed to bring their intellect to bear on matters of faith.

A series of events caught my attention and culminated in my acknowledgment that some force greater than humanity existed in creation. I was on a quest to add purpose to my life, pondering what mattered most to me. Studying quantum physics was most helpful in "cracking the code" of our cosmos, adding a fresh perspective to our existence. At the same time, I headed a task force to provide meaningful summer experiences for special kids. As I pulled together business, churches, synagogues, and foundations, I watched something bigger than the sum of the parts at work. People who usually fought each other tooth and nail down at City Hall were cooperating. Supplies arrived like magic, major obstacles dissolved, and I thought, "This is God. I may be a leader, but God's hand is on this undertaking." Understanding even a part of God could take a lifetime, but I'm determined to pursue adding a spiritual dimension to my life.
—Stan, 53, human resources consultant

With this outlook, Extraverted Thinking types find discrepancies and disputable matters. Unexamined beliefs or dogmas have no place in Extraverted Thinking spirituality.

Prayer

For Extraverted Thinking types, prayer might involve acting to change structures that seem corrupt or unfair. Often their prayer is objectively honest about their own faith and doubts. More likely they use their head than their heart when they pray.

- The prayer of Extraverted Thinking types is quite different from that of the other types as they often take a dispassionate, cerebral approach.

  I conceptualize prayer as a reflecting-meditating behavior as akin to other thought processes but without the extreme logical sequences. It's a piece of the mind that also embraces the heart and the spirit. In other words, yes we are Thinkers, but that doesn't separate our prayers from the more affective components of the Spirit.
  —Matt, 42, corporate manager

- Their conversations with God may be as questioning or confrontational in style as other aspects of their spiritual journey. The biblical Job is a good example of skeptical and challenging prayer.

- They often seek a solid purpose for prayer. When that purpose is lacking, prayer life can be weakened or even extinguished. Author Bruce Duncan in *Pray Your Way* describes it as a form of prayer that never lets you forget that "God calls you to responsible concern for social justice and that political awareness and activity are imperatives for Christians."
- Some Extraverted Thinking types follow a set prayer ritual, using suggestions from a knowledgeable source or a book of prayers.

As I read the morning paper, I literally count my blessings and consider if I should apply my skills to any of the problems the news describes and add these to my prayers.
—Dustin, 56, attorney

Worship

For Extraverted Thinking types, joining a church or synagogue allows them to be a part of a force larger than themselves that can be used to correct injustices and solve problems.

- Often Extraverted Thinking types approach their worship life in a manner similar to the way they approach the rest of their lives: pragmatically and purposefully. They often look to spirituality to build a moral foundation for themselves and their families, to widen their social circles, or to provide important traditions and rituals. These goals may lead them to join spiritual communities or other environments that address these issues.

It's not a deliberate process, nor is it as organized as the rest of my life. While I pursue private soulwork to gain more understanding of my spirituality, too much pressure to explain all these inner thoughts or share on a personal level is difficult for me. Many people don't suspect or know just how spiritual I am because I'm uncomfortable with the unknown aspects of it.
—Marissa, 52, small business owner

- Introspection, meditation, and contemplation within worship help Extraverted Thinking types build a personal relationship with God.
- Their rigorous honesty safeguards against superstition. If a sermon or ritual only tugs at emotions, they find it shallow. They don't

want to concentrate on God's love at the expense of understanding God's plans for justice, responsibility, and righteousness.

Study

For Extraverted Thinking types, study is often done in formal learning settings such as church classes, seminaries, or university courses. Their spirituality demands examination, challenge, and critical thinking.

- Extraverted Thinking types often learn by asking "big questions," seeking intellectual challenge, and discussing paradoxes with others who want to use a disciplined inquiry to explore theological questions. Often their most spiritual moments come when they are allowed to bring their intellect to bear on matters of faith.

My first Hebrew instructor deserved every bit of the respect he demanded. He was very competent and that made it easy for me to accept his moral stance and teaching. However, his example provides an extremely high benchmark for me to judge other spiritual leaders and movements. When they don't measure up, I can easily become skeptical and question the purpose of belonging or participating fully.
  —Beth, 26, graduate student

- Extraverted Thinking types attend structured programs or classes that deal with "hard issues" both practical and philosophical.

The goals for my spiritual life have to be as conquerable as the goals in other areas of my life. I need a course to complete, a book to finish reading, a specific plan for spiritual growth so I know when and if I've met my goal.
  —Greta, 36, homemaker

- Intellectually-oriented Bible study (or another holy book) attracts Extraverted Thinking types who use it to inform or influence their faith and personal principles.

I love the traditions in which I was raised, but I tend not to look to them for all the rules concerning right or wrong that many people have about faith. Rather, I try to define the bigger picture of the characteristics of a faith-filled person.
  —Deanna, 36, personnel manager

Service

Extraverted Thinking types work first to define principles, then to define purpose, and finally to evaluate whether a service opportunity both matters and is effective. Their outward, goal-oriented leadership—running committees, chairing service projects, or otherwise being responsible to their community—is often spiritually motivated.

- Extraverted Thinking types want the world to be organized according to logical principles and, therefore, often find themselves in leadership or administrative roles for projects where tangible or future-oriented good works can be accomplished efficiently or problems solved effectively.

I have always been a part of the system and see value in what "the church" has to offer. However, the traditional ways used to reach a wide array of people (including myself) have not been very effective. While out of one side of my mouth I will say that "church" is not for me (meaning those traditional methods), on the other hand I say, "If only we did it this way, or in this setting, or with this leadership, etc., it would be more effective." Somehow I see the bigger picture, understand the underlying purpose, and suggest or develop new strategies to meet the end goal. I've been able to do this in several capacities within my denomination and it truly brings me joy.
—Tani, 31, minister

- Many Extraverted Thinking types like to work with the finances of an organization, making sure that funds are dispersed according to priorities, schedules, and overall goals.
- Extraverted Thinking types also use their natural skeptical and critical natures to evaluate programs, policies, and plans. Finding the flaws and correcting them is a key way for them to be of service.

It's just part of how I am made. In my spiritual community, I join with others to brainstorm on all of the issues we could attack—fetal alcohol syndrome, migrant workers, inner-city crime—we choose which ones we can influence, we develop a plan, and then we go out and do something about it! I can't do these things alone and therefore appreciate my effectiveness as part of a social-outreach unit.
—Phyllis, 42, financial planner

Other Forms of Soulwork

With their love of logic, Extraverted Thinking types find many ways to tap into their spiritual side through questioning and debating their faith, seeking clear examples of faith in action, and leading efforts to make a difference in their worlds.

- Extraverted Thinking types can often focus on God in settings of grandeur, whether the cathedrals of civilization, or forests, mountains, or seashores. Their surroundings foster awareness of the power of God in their lives.
- Extraverted Thinking types like to determine moral and ethical standards. They often use logical, established religious systems as a base and then define their own principles. The result can be a life purpose that guides their efforts toward something that matters.

I struggle with capital punishment and gender issues. They can seem absolute. We need a right and wrong, but when you're dealing with people, those areas get pretty gray. Still, I want a standard to compare against—and the right to voice my informed opinion.
   —Henry, 53, service-agency director

- Many Extraverted Thinking types like to go to retreats, rallies, or other large spiritual gatherings. While they may shy away if everyone is expected to share feelings, they do seek intellectual stimulation and an understanding of the effects of faith in the lives of others.

In short, Extraverted Thinking spirituality helps all of us remember that
- defining and clarifying truth and universal principles are important,
- intellectual and philosophical inquiries foster new answers to spiritual questions,
- systems and beliefs need to be examined with logic and universal frameworks,
- doubts are catalysts in searching for new understanding.

The Second Half of Life's Spiritual Journey

While Extraverted Thinking is about skepticism and searching for clarity and truth, eventually Extraverted Thinking types feel the need to look at what matters to them and those they care about. They also ponder what legacy they want to leave to others. If they continue to distance themselves from their emotional life, what will they have missed?

Often at this stage, Extraverted Thinking types have developed their natural spiritual path. Then, richness and depth come through their inferior function, Introverted Feeling. This involves

- searching for the personal meaning in spiritual practices;
- having an inner bedrock of values to determine what is important, then attempting to live in accordance with those values;
- finding time for solitary and deep soulwork and paying attention to the joys and longings of the spiritual journey;
- cultivating close personal relationships—first with self, then with selected others by sharing feelings and matters of the heart.

While they may continue many of their favorite methods of soulwork, here are some examples of what Extraverted Thinking types found as they journeyed on into Introverted Feeling:

Emotions were always some sort of an unknown black box for me, so to speak. Now I'm intrigued by the notion that emotions are things we do, not things that just happen to us. They are a valuable part of experiencing all that life has to offer, not something to avoid at all costs.

For me, God was always "out there." Now I find the visionary writings of people like St. Teresa of Avila and some of the Eastern mystics fascinating.

Until recently I considered journaling unimportant and a waste of good time. However, I've started a process of writing down those things that are truly significant to me. Through this journal, I can be sure that my time goes to what is most important.

At just the right moment, someone handed me a values exercise. What really did matter to me? I had my goals, my mission statement, but suddenly that wasn't enough. The people side of my life wasn't adequately represented. While I value using my talents to the fullest, I also value time with those I love, laughter, and—of all things—leisure!

In Africa, working in solitude on a technical assignment, I had more time than at any other point in my life to reflect on what brings meaning to me—no phones, no TV, no newspapers to provide information.

Without distractions, I felt the presence of God in a new and very deep way. I realized that I wanted to live for a purpose; if I listened, perhaps my spiritual side could enable me to be a force to improve our world—at least the small part I can influence.

Any of the Introverted Feeling pathways (chapter 10) can bring this kind of rest and richness for Extraverted Thinking types, if they allow their dominant functions a time of rest and let the Spirit guide their thoughts and actions.

ESTJ

Extraversion Sensing Thinking Judging

Spirituality in the outer world of principles and action

Be diligent in these matters; give yourself wholly to them.
—1 Timothy 4:15

Greatest Gifts

Uncovering truth and seeking justice through objective and efficient problem-solving

Moving quickly toward accomplishing practical and necessary tasks

Role in Community

Leading people and processes toward tangible accomplishments and goals in a responsible, methodical way to make the most of a situation, task, or plan

---

ESTJs tend to be decisive, to-the-point, and practical organizers who value accomplishment and closure. They use logical analysis to guide their actions. They enjoy being in charge, directing others, and providing structure while monitoring their own and the group's commitments. They are forceful and systematic.

Using their dominant function, Extraverted Thinking, is the natural starting place for soulwork. However, their auxiliary or second function, *Introverted Sensing*, calls them to pull back for introspection.

Soulwork through the Second Function

Introverted Sensing helps ESTJs determine their own practical spiritual needs and to see if their choices are in line with the facts of the situation.

ESTJs can also engage their Introverted Sensing function by structuring time for reflective spiritual disciplines. They may choose to engage in time-honored practices, such as following the suggestions in a book of prayer or designing a personal ritual that they use regularly.

> *After putting all my energy for several months toward pursuing an advanced degree, I had to get away by myself to rethink my situation. I realized that I hadn't given enough thought to whether this profession would allow me to live my life by my principles. Was this the right educational track for me? Did my skills match the career requirements? Was it worth the time investment? While I eventually decided that I was on the right path, this pause to reevaluate all the details and facts gave me the confidence I needed to move ahead.*
> —Ashley, 25, MBA student

ESTJs can enhance their spirituality by using their senses—sights, sounds, and aromas—for soulwork. Introverted Sensing also calls them to slow their pace and pay attention to their body's needs (diet, exercise, rest). Monitoring their physical state can also provide them with a mirror of their own emotions.

> *I stop myself, quiet down, and look at what hurts. For example, when my stomach gets irritable, I know it's a clue for me to take it easy and determine the real source of my frustration. The answer often comes quickly. Then I can use this information to plan actions to rectify the situation.*
> —Carla, 28, probation officer

Within these settings, ESTJs might seek to use Introverted Sensing by engaging in any of the exercises listed for Sensing (pages 49-52), with goals such as

- appreciating the richness of spiritual traditions;
- reflecting on the past and present to apply soulwork to practical, personal service;
- focusing on their internal experiences, needs, and realities;
- noticing the fullness of detail in the real world;
- examining the facts and what experience has taught them.

All of these might help them bring clarity to their beliefs and depth to their soulwork.

What Might Push ESTJs Away from Their Spiritual Path

With their drive to find consistency and truth, ESTJs can easily find fuel for doubt and skepticism along their spiritual path. Common themes we heard from ESTJs we interviewed included

- observing a violation of accepted codes of conduct, either by those in leadership positions or by a change in the rules. ESTJs may struggle to support any group that fails to be fair or to hold its leader accountable.
- desiring proof to ascertain their spiritual reality.

  There are no facts, nothing is certain. Part of me believes in heaven, yet part of me wonders whether there really is anything beyond our life here. This knowledge gives me a zest for making this life count. However, as I'm learning and growing more in my faith and getting older, I'm more drawn to sort out what I truly believe.
  —William, 45, vice president of administration

- not seeing any material benefits from spirituality.

  I find it very easy to ignore the call of my spiritual side. Bills demand to be paid, work projects must be completed, and I devote a considerable amount of energy to community service through my men's club. I do my part and follow my principles in so many aspects of life that I wonder if soulwork is necessary.
  —Ted, 51, executive

- being asked to depart radically from the tried and true in spiritual practices or disciplines. ESTJs prefer to stay with what is already known and tend not to want to tamper with important truths or traditions.

Trusted spiritual advisors, friends, and family can help ESTJs find an enriching spiritual path by

- working to help them accomplish tasks that they could not do alone,
- reminding them that nothing can be efficient all the time and that in inefficiency and chaos something valuable might be gained,

- persuading them to try a spiritual approach by outlining its benefits and practical applications to their situation,
- helping them appreciate life's intangibles by remembering the times when they were in awe of what God has done.

When Life Is Difficult

The fourth, or *inferior*, function for ESTJs is Introverted Feeling. With their emphasis on logic and objectivity, tapping into the Introverted Feeling realm of values and subjectivity is a struggle. In times of stress, the inferior function can erupt, changing the ESTJ's behavior into a caricature of ISFPs and INFPs for whom it is the *dominant* function.

For ESTJs in times of stress, the following circumstances might trigger the inferior function:

- When they begin to doubt their ability to cope with the situation. For ESTJs, who value a regulated approach to life, this loss of control can be especially threatening. Knowing that their logic and problem-solving skills are not matched or able to "best" the problem, they can be moved to quit.
- When they are expected to lead during a crisis but have already reached their limit. Because ESTJs habitually take charge, others expect them to continue to do so even in times of loss. However, ESTJs may want to be taken care of themselves, may seek to withdraw to avoid any emotional displays, or may reluctantly assume, at a personal cost, their normal leadership role.

  Because so much was coming so fast, I knew if I continued, I would start shouting, "I'm being treated like a robot!" or "It's not fair; others aren't helping!" I had to get away for a solo bike ride and a good cup of coffee but felt instead like I was shirking my responsibilities.
  —Gwen, 35, insurance investigator

- When a deeply rooted principle is disregarded or violated by themselves or others.
- When they, in some way, may have inadvertently hurt people. In their drive toward accomplishment, ESTJs may have to face up to what others perceive as impatient, cold, or unfeeling actions. This can be debilitating, especially if ESTJs thought they were acting in the best interests of all. In most crises, ESTJs continue to focus on the external problems, giving rather limited time to

emotional states—their own or others' needs for consolation or support. Sometimes it takes a significant intervention by others or their conscience before they slow down enough to consider the impact of the situation.

Often, the worst times for ESTJs are when they become driven to succeed only to find their efforts inefficient or useless. Perhaps they overused their dominant function, Thinking, by becoming so caught up in their chosen, logical plan or decision that they closed themselves to new information and ignored the other aspects of the crisis—the interpersonal, long-range, or factual implications. In addition, if they haven't focused on soulwork in the past, ESTJs may overlook the spiritual dimension of their crisis situation. When everything becomes too personal and emotionally sensitive, their inferior function, Feeling, takes on a dark cast.

> *When I was fired, my first reaction was shock. I focused on what others had done to cause it—the lack of management planning, the inefficient sales force, etc. As I started my job search, I had to come to grips with the issues where I could be at fault: my business and my interpersonal skills. Only after much introspection did I pinpoint those areas that need development. I was surprised by my emotional response because I had damaged a number of important work relationships. I found an excellent executive coach and started immediately to modify my behavior by considering people and goals.*
> —Ryan, 44, manufacturing manager

In these situations, ESTJs might be uncharacteristically overemotional or hypersensitive. Or they might concentrate too intently on the tasks at hand, acting cold and impersonal toward others. When these symptoms appear, a totally different approach to soulwork often helps. ESTJs might *purposefully* pursue Introverted Feeling. Its *conscious use* requires ESTJs to shut down what is usually easiest—Extraverted Thinking—which may have gotten out of control. By doing so, ESTJs can look at the interpersonal aspects of a given situation and reflect on questions about what is most important for themselves, others, and society.

Ways to intentionally engage the Introverted Feeling function include
- paying attention to the emotional impact of a situation by setting aside all of its demands and concentrating on the personal meaning

of what has happened. This affective information becomes input in the decision-making process.

- stepping back from the logical implications to consider what effect their selected outcome has on those closest to them. ESTJs often find it rather unnatural to consciously explore these areas. Therefore, they may find it easier to talk things through with an empathetic listener whom they trust.

- engaging in reflective recreational opportunities that allow them to express their inner feelings or to contemplate motivations. Possibilities include painting, writing, reading literature or poetry, or journaling.

In the chosen activity, the key is backing away from uncontrolled emotionalism and instead focusing on caring about themselves and others. As one ESTJ put it, "I was afraid I'd cry, but I decided if that occurred, I could handle it. I mustered up my courage and told my aging parents how much I loved them. I also went on to delineate what they'd done for me and my appreciation for it all. To my delight and surprise, we all cried, hugged, and felt closer than ever. I was so glad I took the risk."

As an ESTJ, I am thankful for
    my orientation toward fairness and justice,
    my sense of order and responsibility,
    my ability to lead others to accomplish goals,
    the decisiveness and reasoning I bring to solving problems.

When life is difficult, I can find support by
    focusing on what truly matters to me, both now and for eternity;
    embracing instead of avoiding my emotions, realizing that feelings can enrich my life;
    taking time alone to ensure that *all* my needs are met.

To honor myself and my pathway to God, I can
    find tangible ways to incorporate the spiritual into my daily life,
    use my organizational gifts to be a part of something that matters,
    value the intangible—my relationships and other areas that give meaning to life.

ENTJ

Extraversion Intuition Thinking Judging

Spirituality in the outer world of objectivity and possibilities

Dear children, let us not love with words or tongue but with actions and in truth.
—1 John 3:18

Greatest Gifts
Bringing order out of chaos, stepping into voids requiring leadership and vision
Energetically mobilizing others to action to meet needs for posterity

Role in Community
Long-range planning and envisioning future-oriented ideas
Calling others to competence
Decisive leadership for groups and organizations
Bringing intellectual and philosophical insights to spiritual questions

---

ENTJs tend to be active, take-charge organizers of processes, people, and plans. They are goal-directed, big-picture focused, and ardent problem-solvers, especially of large and complex issues. They enjoy providing structure and designing strategies to correct systems. ENTJs have high expectations, are persistent, and value fairness.

Using their dominant function, Extraverted Thinking, is the natural starting place for soulwork. However, their auxiliary or second function,

Introverted Intuition, calls them to focus on future possibilities, delve into the unseen, and contemplate life's big questions.

Soulwork through the Second Function

Introverted Intuition points ENTJs toward other interpretations and applications of their principles and beliefs. Pulling back from their active lifestyle to reflect on possibilities can add depth to their soulwork.

Rather than total solitude for reflection, ENTJs might take part in family, social, or recreational pursuits that help them find opportunities for their Intuition. Many ENTJs find that solitude allows them to pay attention to the insights and hunches they received through their Intuition.

> *Once I recharge, tell me it can't be done and all my energy will go to finding a way to make it happen, bringing others along for the ride. After a period of time, I need to slow down, refocus, and recharge the battery—even for a short, short while—then it's back to high gear again.*
> —Ellen, 29, executive recruiter

Some ENTJs schedule time for exploring things or events that cannot be easily explained through logic or reason. They tend to come up with better possibilities for solutions when alone—perhaps when pursuing their daily tasks.

Within these settings, ENTJs might seek to use Introverted Intuition by engaging in any of the exercises listed for Intuition (pages 94-98), with goals such as

- reflecting about problems and solutions;
- working to identify several options to reach a goal;
- considering the interrelationships between the parts and the whole;
- paying attention to important insights and hunches they receive through daydreaming, prayer, or meditation;
- getting enough sleep to foster fresh ideas and optimism.

All of these might help them bring clarity to their beliefs and depth to their soulwork.

> *I've learned to trust my intuition in spiritual matters. When I take the time to meditate over a situation the answer often becomes palpably clear. There's no logic or thought involved—I just know what I am supposed to do or pass on to another person. The rightness of this*

is confirmed when others tell me that God put me in their life for a reason. Allowing my intuition to guide me helps me move past some of the demands of my Thinking function.

—Kent, 64, investment banker

What Might Push ENTJs Away from Their Spiritual Path

When logic is violated or if ENTJs are not affirmed for their competencies, their desire to search for truth in their spiritual underpinnings may be weakened or even extinguished. Common themes we heard from ENTJs we interviewed included

- with their natural drive to solve problems set before them, ENTJs usually find objective, rational, and complex solutions, then move ahead with confidence. When these solutions are not adopted, ENTJs can feel undervalued.
- perceiving a lack of purpose in some forms of spirituality. With the many other purposeful activities in which ENTJs engage, spirituality may then be relegated to a low priority in their lives.
- demanding competency in all aspects of their life from themselves and others and being disenchanted by its occasional absence within organized religion. While ENTJs can be found at the forefront of many spiritual endeavors, taking the leap of faith from a life of logic to a life of belief can be a difficult step for many.
- avoiding situations that bring out aspects of emotion, either from themselves or others. Too much talk of love, relationships, and feelings can push ENTJs away from spiritual pathways.

Part of it might be that I just don't use some of the language that is common to many spiritual paths. If I say that I'm influenced by the traditions of a given community, agree with its basic theological tenants, and can commit myself to acting on its priorities—well, that is passionate language for me. I think in terms of purposes and results as I seek my spiritual path, not personal relationships and feeling loved.

—Paul, 44, real estate developer

Trusted spiritual advisors, friends, and family can help ENTJs find an enriching spiritual path by

- offering them opportunities to slow down and "waste time" on social interactions;
- joining with them in challenging traditional thoughts, dogmas, and paradigms;
- recognizing that for ENTJs faith is more logical than emotional;
- understanding that for ENTJs the spiritual journey can be a very personal thing and may not be readily influenced by others.

When Life Is Difficult

The fourth or *inferior* function for ENTJs is Introverted Feeling. With their emphasis on clarifying principles of faith through rigorous study, debate, and discussion, ENTJs can struggle when focusing on intrapersonal meaning. In times of stress, the inferior function can erupt, changing the ENTJ's behavior into a caricature of ISFPs and INFPs for whom the Feeling function is the *dominant* function.

For ENTJs in times of stress, the following circumstances might trigger the inferior function:

- When they believe their own lack of spiritual or intellectual competency may have contributed to a poor outcome.

  As a religious professional I wanted to be competent at all aspects of my work, but providing personal counseling to members of our spiritual community was problematic for me. I took classes only to learn that many counseling sessions were doomed to fail—people often seek counseling in religious settings because they don't want to change! I finally learned that competency in this area doesn't necessarily mean that people solve their problems or that I must do it for them.
  —Zachary, 48, rabbi

- When they or those close to them lose control over their emotions.
- When others construe their actions as treating people like objects or interchangeable parts.

  I didn't mean to discredit other people, but I was in such a "Just do it!" mode that I moved too quickly past the people part of the process. I had to go back to several of the staff members to double check how they had interpreted my comments—and it was not an enjoyable incident.
  —Lynne, 41, corporate executive

- When a spiritual principle or truth is disregarded or violated. Because of their thoughtful and considered approach to spirituality, when ENTJs choose to commit to a spiritual path or tradition, they can be annoyed when others sweep spiritual principles aside.

Often the worst time for ENTJs is when their own abilities fail them and a sense of powerlessness sets in. Perhaps they have overused their dominant function, Thinking, by reducing everything to a logical formula—even though many of life's issues are illogical. When these dark times come, ENTJs may quickly become frustrated.

> On the one hand, I knew my spouse should be frightened and even tearful as we waited for the results of the medical tests. On the other hand, though, I found myself wanting to avoid any interaction with him and the doctors until we could have a rational, unemotional discussion of how to proceed. So I felt cold, guilty, and useless to help.
> —Sandy, 38, attorney

In these situations, ENTJs might be uncharacteristically rigid in their approach to problems and unwilling to see other possibilities. They might be self-pitying, illogical, or emotional. When these symptoms appear, a totally different approach to soulwork often helps. ENTJs might *purposefully* pursue Introverted Feeling. Its *conscious use* requires ENTJs to shut down what is usually easiest—Extraverted Thinking—which may have gotten out of control. By doing so, ENTJs can slow down and take stock of their deepest principles to see if these are reflected in their actions. They may also find a trusted person to provide an outside viewpoint on how people are being affected by the ENTJ's actions.

Ways to consciously engage the Feeling function include

- completing a values-clarification exercise to determine what matters to them personally. Sometimes this helps ENTJs select efforts that have the most meaning from the many possible challenges they have the ability to tackle.
- stepping back from the logical implications of a situation to consider the impact the ENTJ's solution has on those closest to them. They might also pay attention to their own feelings and emotional states about the situation and use them as factors in their decision-making.
- reading novels or journaling to get at issues of character and motivation; painting or writing poetry to express inner emotions; or

talking one-to-one with a trusted other about deeply personal matters.

The key for ENTJs is to realize, in their chosen activity, the impact of decisions on people; to pay attention to their own emotional state; and to clarify and honor their own spiritual values. One ENTJ said, "My crisis made me look at faith in a new way. No, I couldn't provide intellectual proof. However, there *is* something out there bigger and more competent than I am. I found support and perhaps even tenderness or love from what I term 'God.'"

As an ENTJ, I am thankful for
> my mind that sees solutions and strategies where others see turmoil,
> my quest for truth and clarity, adding insights to each endeavor,
> my commitment to excellence in everything I undertake,
> the way I lead people toward well-defined goals.

When life is difficult, I can find support by
> taking time out to explore alternative possibilities and solutions,
> discovering what matters most to me and to those I value,
> considering the experiences of others and asking for their help.

To honor myself and my pathway to God, I can
> satisfy my need to know—my desire to understand our universe and ultimately our Creator,
> define and accept a logical basis for what I take on faith—be able to intellectualize this intangible part of our being,
> find ways to bring my soulwork to bear on my relationships with others and with God.

CHAPTER EIGHT

INTROVERTED THINKING:

*The Conceptual
Spiritual Path*

Introverted Thinking Spirituality
ISTP, INTP

*Observing, analyzing, and searching for underlying principles,
double standards, and hypocrisy.
Connecting soulwork to the quest for truth and deep understanding
of the spiritual nature of people and the universe.*

O ur first conversations with Introverted Thinking types about what draws them toward God and what pushed them away helped us clarify our goals for *SoulTypes*. They were quick to ask, "What do you mean by spirituality? What do you hope to learn? For you, what is God?" Apparently our eventual answers struck a chord with these types; they provided the longest responses we received—six- and seven-page single-spaced e-mails detailing their early religious experiences and their frustrations. Or, from those who lived in our city, lunch meetings that extended into late afternoon as they realized we really wanted their opinions!

Introverted Thinking types are not easily persuaded by traditional dogmas or rituals of spirituality. They know that there are no easy answers to life's big questions and are uneasy when people try to assume away life's dilemmas. As one Introverted Thinking type told us:

> My beliefs are the product of my mind. The more trappings that are added, the harder it is for me to believe. Take Moses and the burning bush, the parting of the Red Sea—the story starts to sound like any Greek or Roman myth. Embellishments like angels and miracles make me think twice—I wonder whether I've placed my faith in another string of legends.
>
> While these stories can be historical, they could also be God-inspired vehicles designed to make us think and ponder the divine aspects of life. In addition, the alternative is atheism, and . . . well, you don't shake off years of attending religious services. My faith provides a structure for day-to-day reality.
> —Debra, 49, nurse

For most Introverted Thinking types, soulwork is a rational process. They may not be easily convinced of its merits without thought and logic. With their healthy natural skepticism, they seek spiritual environments that welcome doubts. If they find the topic of spirituality interesting—and not all Introverted Thinking types do—they voice their questions, viewing them as spurs for spiritual inquiry. For many, this is the most captivating part of spirituality.

Not content with the definitions of others, Introverted Thinkers seek to define their own spirituality by setting up logical principles and steps to prove or disprove different spiritual truths. They also work to explain things that fail to meet logical criteria. When questioned, they offer a rationale for their approach, finding the most sensible or most comprehensive explanation. Most give well-reasoned arguments or justifications of their positions, not personal opinions.

> My parents were really narrow-minded: you take one path or the other. As a youth I did a quick pro-and-con analysis and figured that religion would probably do me more good than harm, so I went along with it. Now that I've been involved for years, I see much

finer nuances than my original logic, but that's initially what got me here!

    —Tara, 27, occupational therapist

Introverted Thinking types are also keen observers of people and notice how their spirituality influences their lives. In part, they base their decisions about different spiritual traditions or "spiritual" people on this type of evidence. They run the gamut from deeply-committed religious leaders to atheists. At either extreme, they do not suffer fools gladly.

Occasionally, a sense of spiritual inadequacy can creep in because Introverted Thinkers eschew the more interpersonal (some would say "touchy-feely") aspects of many spiritual traditions. Witnessing for the faith, open demonstrations of emotions, and public discussions of private matters—spiritual practices that some people view as essential—can be hard on the private Introverted Thinking types.

I grew up as a preacher's kid. I was constantly mortified when members of my dad's congregation would say, "Let's hear a witness from the preacher's son!" At the first chance of leaving the charade, I opted for independence and left the community for good.

    —Leroy, 53, editor

When any such pressure to conform exists, many Introverted Thinking types, because of their desire to be true to their principles, leave rather than submit. When they do "find religion," they continue to challenge traditions to get at the underlying truths. Many religious writers, teachers, and preachers of note are Introverted Thinking types.

Prayer

For most Introverted Thinking types, prayer is a private matter. They choose methods that match their love of reflection, observation, and the life of the mind.

- Introverted Thinking types may find meditation, contemplation, and prayer more effective in outdoor surroundings.

I have to acknowledge my own spiritual path—soulwork—happens for me when I'm out fishing or hiking. The river is my cathedral, a place where I sense the awesomeness of God.

    —Collin, 33, systems analyst

- Prayer for Introverted Thinking types is also a time and place where they can argue with God about all the problems and inconsistencies between faith and reason.

  I came to know God by losing arguments during prayer. Faith came when I realized I'd never be able to rationally understand all that my spiritual path implied.
    —Courtney, 32, psychologist

- They also like to ponder the inexplicable or identify a sense of order or purpose in an event. Experiences like these often are underpinnings for their faith.
- Some Introverted Thinking types use prayer to reconcile current events with their faith. Because they value truth among all things, they may find themselves analyzing their own lives and where they may have fallen short. How can they rectify their failures?

Worship

Introverted Thinking types want worship to be an avenue that opens up intellectual inquiry and reflection. Traditional worship may fall short of their standards.

- Introverted Thinking spirituality tends to be private, although these types may seek community with others in order to connect, debate, and learn. When they do incorporate worship services into their spiritual path it is because they have found a place that respects their particular way of thinking.

  I find it difficult to be spiritual in the midst of a crowd. Solitude is more refreshing. A few weeks ago I joined with others from my spiritual community to attend a huge gathering. While I enjoyed the opening ritual, I could go for months without another similar experience.
    —Collin 33, systems analyst

- Some Introverted Thinking types are conversant about spirituality without developing personal beliefs. They might even belong to a church and participate in its social outreach yet disagree with its major spiritual tenets. Others might perceive a major inconsistency, but INTPs can place principles in categories, tolerating the discrepancy because of an underlying principle.

- Worship has to show tangible or theoretical results or it loses its value. Worship is most valuable to them when it has an impact on problems and issues facing them, others, or the community or when it links them to people in a special way.

I know that I expect a great deal from any formal expression of spirituality. While any corporate worship experience must engage my mind, it is also logical that a religious belief system should have a strong sense of feeling. I am disappointed in any gathering that is too cognitive. I want to be inspired and uplifted as well.
    —Grant, 45, management professor

Study

Study comes naturally to Introverted Thinking types *when* they have an interest in the subject at hand.

- Introverted Thinking types enjoy knowledgeable discussions where they can "unpack" a spiritual principle, book, or code. They evaluate what is spiritual, the role of faith in people's lives, and the nature of God. Some like classes that bring spirituality to bear on down-to-earth applications like workplace ethics or parenting.
- Reading about spiritual giants may enhance their spirituality, but only if that reading is in context of the time that person lived, has modern parallels to the current situation or issue, or provides information that is either practical or aids in the formation of their guiding spiritual principles.
- They also enjoy wrestling with issues of faith and examining experiences that defy rational explanations. As one Introverted Thinking type said, "We all need to understand what we're buying into and recognize how watered down, emotional, simplistic, or reductionist our faith can be." They might enjoy meeting with a few people for open discussion and questioning of their differing beliefs and for a bit of debate to help with clarification of those beliefs.

In one of my favorite spiritual experiences, we all studied the same subject, discussed information we had learned, and then together assessed what it all meant. I'm more comfortable with spiritual matters that cannot be determined if I've done my best to find the limits of what can be proved. Some people get offended when I ask questions that to me are obvious ones to ask, claiming that I am attacking the core of what they believe. It would be nice if spiritual matters were that clear cut, but they simply aren't. When I admit what I don't know for sure—only then can I identify what I know to be true!

—Ben, 52, telecommunications manager

Service

For Introverted Thinking types, being of service is only a logical extension of a system of beliefs. Through community, they can find formal services or social outreach programs to act out their faith principles.

- When they perceive injustice or a lack of fairness, Introverted Thinking types often try to identify the problem and then provide the resources to help. They then expect people who espouse a belief in service to step forward and assist. While they do not typically take direct leadership roles, they do lend their ideas and support and usually stay with endeavors until they are completed.

- Many Introverted Thinking types assist with setting up and maintaining automation, computerization, or audio-visual systems, making sure that the most effective and efficient systems are used.

- Introverted Thinking types contribute either a hands-on or a heads-up type of service. Some jump in to help in crises or other situations where physical talents are needed; others offer a blueprint for a service or ministry.

I think of it this way: God and I have a contract. My part is to do what I can for others and God's part is to influence what I do. I don't expect answers for every little problem I face, but I believe that if I am committed to a faithful life, acting on my principles, then God provides direction by guiding my thoughts. I don't have a need to ask for more.

—Greg, 27, forester

Other Forms of Soulwork

With their love of the life of the mind and their quest for truth, Introverted Thinking types find quiet and deep ways to express their spirituality.

- Introverted Thinkers may take time away from a structured spiritual system to define for themselves what spirituality means and find spiritual practices that honor their love of reflection.

  When others try to tell me that faith is about believing, I point out that there is no sense believing what isn't true. For me, the question as to whether the stories of my religious tradition are true or not is irrelevant. Whether they are myth or fact, what is important is the truth in their meaning and insights into human nature.
  —Ellen, 59, psychologist

- Academic or practical pursuits, from philosophy to fly-fishing, can inform the Introverted Thinker's faith. They may look for ways their beliefs can improve parenting or how their other interests can inform their theology.
- For many Introverted Thinking types, soulwork is service. Proof of its reality is whether people *act.* They look for God in human interactions, observing whether faith is making a difference.

In short, Introverted Thinking spirituality helps us all remember that

- choosing one's spiritual path through an objective process of examination is worth doing;
- raising doubts brings clarity to spiritual issues and usually indicates an interest in the subject being raised;
- searching for guiding universal principles is helpful to all spiritualities;
- defining what is true and setting standards built on that truth make spirituality more viable and cogent in today's world.

The Second Half of Life's Journey

While Introverted Thinking is about determining truth, eventually life grows short. Or, as do all personalities, Introverted Thinking types begin to wonder whether they have found sufficient meaning and purpose.

Often at this stage, the Introverted Thinking types have developed their natural spiritual path. Then, richness comes through the inferior function, Extraverted Feeling. This involves

- discerning what is of most importance to people in their environment, especially those closest to them;
- joining with others in community to accomplish tasks that are helpful for individuals and society;
- reaching out and communicating warmth and affection to others;
- focusing on what is positive in spiritual pathways, leaders, and sacred texts, and noting what is worthy of gratitude and appreciation.

While Introverted Thinking types may continue many of their favorite methods of soulwork, here are some examples of what they found as they journeyed on into Extraverted Feeling:

> Time with those I care about is now equally as important as the solitary moments I've always needed. I've sought help for my tendency to close myself off from others because I don't want to repeat the patterns of my family of origin. I've learned to express my feelings in ways that don't seem manipulative or forced.

> As a child, religious times meant little more to me than our house was overrun by noisy relatives. Now I look forward to those times when we gather to worship in one place. Preparing the special foods that we eat during these times and using the traditions that came from our grandmother make me aware of the way our attendance at worship binds our family together.

> I spent years proving or disproving every tenant of my faith, seldom letting the message sink in. "Feeling" God's love was a foreign concept. Then one day my spiritual director asked, "Do you think God loves you?" "Yes, all my analyses add up to that." "But do you really believe that?" He suggested that I catalog the times I had felt the love of others and how many times I had hurt those who love me. I then realized the power of God's love for me. That was the beginning of my new spiritual relationship with God—at the age of 45! I found deep, powerful encounters when I recognized the value of my inner feelings.

> After our father died, I gathered my siblings together. We set aside all of our logical analysis about the benefits of selling the family cabin and discussed how we felt about it! Even though we may only use

the cabin a few weeks of the year, we realized that the memories and traditions were too strong to sever. Sharing it might be a hassle, but we won't sell the cabin!

Pre-midlife, evaluating the emotions of others to show the appropriate response seemed manipulative. I wasn't being my true self, yet being my true self sometimes caused hurt in others. This was a useful ana-lytical tool—internally modeling how others reacted in the past to get information about their likely future behavior. I can now provoke or permit empathy, after I've analyzed the situation intellectually. Part of my soulwork now is learning to occasionally give my emotions free rein—perhaps even shed tears.

Any of the Extraverted Feeling pathways (chapter 9) can bring this kind of rest and richness when Introverted Thinking types allow their dominant functions a time of rest and let the Spirit guide their thoughts and actions.

ISTP

Introversion Sensing Thinking Perceiving

Spirituality in the inner world of questions and experiences

But whoever lives by the truth comes into the light that it may be seen plainly that what he has done has been done through God.
—John 3:21

Greatest Gifts

Analyzing facts and details in a search for truth; Dissolving red tape in the process of finding the best way to get things done

Role in Community

Contributing quietly behind-the-scenes; Lending a hand when no one else steps forward; Offering a wealth of information about their special interests; Providing realism to any effort they undertake

---

ISTPs tend to be reserved observers who use logic and reasoning to find expedient and efficient ways to get things done. They value clarity of thought and are adept problem-solvers who seek pragmatic solutions. ISTPs prefer to remain in the background unless there are extenuating circumstances—then they act quickly to come to the rescue.

Using the dominant function, Introverted Thinking, is the natural starting place for soulwork. However, their auxiliary or second function, *Extraverted Sensing,* calls them to experience the sacred in what is immediate and real while engaging fully in the active life given to us.

Soulwork through the Second Function

Extraverted Sensing helps ISTPs see the spiritual in the world around them and allows them to see more than one point of view as they seek out facts and applications. Extraverted Sensing often fosters a need in ISTPs to gather with others, whether in a small group or a large organization. This second function offers them an opportunity to see the spiritual in the world around them via concrete examples of ways in which soulwork has helped others—what those people did and what happened next as a result.

> *While I would seldom organize a block party or other social event, I devised a rotating schedule for renting log splitters and teaming together with other families to fill everyone's woodsheds. The gatherings were a lot of fun and had a practical purpose.*
> —John, 37, small-business owner

Some ISTPs enjoy spontaneous outings where they can act on their principles in practical ways, seeing common everyday occurrences as a way to tap into their gratitude for life.

Within these settings, Introverted Thinking types might use Extraverted Sensing by engaging in any of the exercises listed in the Extraverted Sensing section (pages 51-52), with goals such as
- seeing tangible evidence of God in the world around them,
- reassessing the facts and givens in a situation,
- examining concrete examples of how faith has helped other people,
- applying spiritual teachings to daily, practical purposes,
- enjoying the straightforward gift of just being alive.

All of these might help ISTPs bring clarity to their beliefs and breadth to their soulwork.

> *At night, I feel closest to the power that some call God. Gazing at the stars that just hint of the vastness of the universe, I long to understand the one who designed this planet.*
> —Brett, 28, carpenter

What Might Push ISTPs Away from Their Spiritual Path

With their need to tap into the search for truth and to have a logical understanding of the world of spirituality, ISTPs seldom fit the mold of what others consider spiritual. Common themes we heard from the ISTPs we interviewed included

- being frustrated by rituals or worship services that lacked substance or practical application. Suggesting that ISTPs be in the same place at the same time each week, following a given course of activities, can feel restrictive and stifling. If ISTPs rebel at the routines insisted upon by others or by religious and cultural norms, their spiritual lives become more accidental or incidental.

- concluding that their spiritual walk is inconsequential compared to that of others. In some circles, mystical experiences or direct personal relationships with God are the benchmark for faith. Rational and often skeptical, ISTPs may assume that if their own lives lack these occurrences, then their soulwork is not authentic.

- perceiving a lack of fairness on the part of spiritual people and institutions. When ISTPs provide resources to help others or organizations to be effective, they expect to see evidence that their assistance made a difference. When needs are identified, they expect people who espouse a belief in service to step forward to assist. ISTPs resent having to do it all or to lead efforts where everyone could have voluntarily cooperated but didn't. When they have these unfair experiences with a group, they may not go back.

- being engulfed by their own emotionalism. ISTPs also resent blatant (or even subtle) attempts of leaders to induce emotionalism or other irrational atmospheres. ISTPs are private people who want to keep their feelings in check.

The "touchy-feely," emotional stuff doesn't work for me. I perceive God as an interconnecting force, not a friend that walks beside me—I simply haven't experienced that. God exists and takes an interest in us, but I don't get hugs from God, nor do I want them. I have my own way of looking at all of this.
—Kori, 63, caterer

Trusted spiritual advisors, friends, and family can help an ISTP find an enriching spiritual path by

- giving tangible, in-the-moment help in time of need, demonstrating a commitment to the greater good;

- reminding the ISTP that not everything, especially people, will be rational;
- providing examples of faith in action, bringing new vantage points to their spiritual perspective;
- allowing brief "time-out" periods from people and from spiritual practices so the ISTPs can be more private and spontaneous.

When Life Is Difficult

The fourth or *inferior* function for the ISTP is Extraverted Feeling. With their emphasis on logic and objectivity, tapping into the Extraverted Feeling realm of warm and supportive relationships, feelings, and harmony can be a struggle.

In times of stress, the inferior function can erupt, changing the ISTP's behavior into a caricature of ENFJs and ESFJs for whom Extraverted Feeling is the *dominant* function. For ISTPs in times of stress, the following circumstances might trigger the inferior function:

- When they are unsure how to handle their own emotional response or that of others.
- When a situation doesn't fit their logical view of what should happen or when they can't grasp the reasons behind events they may become despondent.

  Given that we'd never had a fight, I was clueless as to why my fiancée broke off our relationship. She left town, giving us no chance to discuss her reasons. Alone, my mind spun out of control as I tried to analyze the situation. I found myself longing for affirmation from others and for their assessment that it wasn't all my fault.
  —Chad, 32, police officer

- When the crisis fills their time with too many work activities, family matters, and other concerns requiring their attention. ISTPs then lose the time alone that their dominant Thinking function requires for reflection and energy.
- When they can't find a way to get things done smoothly. ISTPs pride themselves on their ability to step in when needed and provide an efficient way to handle emergencies or crises. When this is not the case, they can feel useless.

My dad should have spent his last days at home but we couldn't reorganize the rooms, order the healthcare equipment, and make the other arrangements fast enough. With my medical background, I should have been able to arrange things, somehow.
    —Lara, 48, HMO administrator

Often the worst of times for ISTPs is when they have analyzed the facts and drawn their own conclusions of the causes and courses of action, closed themselves off from other perspectives, and isolated themselves too much, thereby missing new data that might help them.

My parents didn't want to discuss our differing views on the war. Dad thought I was shirking responsibility. No matter how hard I tried, I couldn't get through to them that my decision was based on months of agonizing analysis of the issues and the results I saw—some of my friends were already dead, the bombs were killing more innocent people than enemies, and I thought our government had lied. When my parents wouldn't even listen, I exploded in a way that shattered my mother. I left feeling that I had lost their love forever. Fortunately, rather than shutting myself off from disagreements that seem too big to surmount, circumstances forced me back home regularly. I took time to see their position and its strengths in a different way. Eventually, I made peace with their point of view. Their principles came from their circumstances, my decision from my own.
    —Tobie, 49, social worker

In these stressful situations, ISTPs may become overly reliant on logic, perhaps splitting hairs. They may refuse to consider new data or overreact to "helpful" suggestions. When these symptoms appear, a totally different approach to soulwork often helps. ISTPs might *purposefully* pursue Extraverted Feeling. Its *conscious use* requires the ISTP to shut down what is usually easiest—Introverted Thinking—which may have gotten out of control. In doing so, the ISTP can interact with people who may bring new data or ways of doing things more efficiently.

Ways to consciously engage the Feeling function include

- selecting projects or enjoyable activities that bring them into community with others.

    I love to cook, but I recently realized that I use my gourmet dinners as a way to relate to other people. I can handle a group of six or eight and we concentrate on the dining experience—the taste, the different textures, and the aromas. The meal is much more enjoyable when shared with a few others.

—Trent, 54, electrical engineer

- completing a values clarification exercise, comparing those values with ones held by significant people in their lives, and factoring subjective criteria into decisions.
- focusing on relationships, being aware of the needs of others, and discovering what is personally meaningful.

In the chosen activity, the key is backing away from uncontrolled emotionalism and instead engaging in a process that makes it worthwhile to pay attention to the impact of spirituality on their values and relationships. As one ISTP put it, "I've come to depend on my Wednesday breakfasts with the 'guys'. All of us are willing to admit the struggles middle age brings. Earlier I wouldn't have cared, but now I want to understand how they are dealing with the issues I also face."

As an ISTP, I am thankful for

my efficiency and ability to get things done,
my quiet commitment to lending a hand when needed,
my reasoning that defines what is,
the practical bent I lend to using systems and information.

When life is difficult, I can find support by

reserving time for reflection and analysis;
finding ways to acknowledge and deal with my emotions;
reassessing reality, reviewing what can and cannot change.

To honor myself and my pathway to God, I can

satisfy my logic and my rational side as I determine my needs for soulwork,
reconsider what I value—the relationships and purposes that will make my life most meaningful,
acknowledge the spiritual in my experience—finding the consistencies and truths that are manifestations of God.

INTP

Introversion Intuition Thinking Perceiving

Spirituality in the inner world of intellect and ideas

And this is my prayer: that your love may abound more and more in knowledge and depth of insight.
—Philippians 1:9

Greatest Gifts
Synthesizing information into logical systems and structures; Analyzing thoughts and ideas; Searching for underlying truths and ethics of fairness to find the best answers to problems

Role in Community
Asking hard questions; Calling attention to inconsistencies; Clarifying positions and categorizing principles; Quietly and deeply exploring issues to provide a blueprint for things in the future

---

INTPs tend to be questors for purity of thought who are motivated to examine universal principles. Focused with intensity on areas that matter to them, INTPs appreciate elegance and effectiveness in the conceptual realm. Independent, resourceful problem-solvers and theoretical model-builders, INTPs relish the life of the mind.

Using their dominant function, Introverted Thinking, is the natural starting place for soulwork. However, their auxiliary or second function,

Extraverted Intuition, calls them to see future possibilities and many connections in the outer world.

Soulwork through the Second Function

INTPs' natural curiosity and need to explore the truth about things leads them into active involvement with people and life. Questioning and debating their insights with others, getting out of the house or workplace, or traveling are favorite ways for INTPs to engage their intuition.

Rather than their soulwork being solely private, INTPs might take part in activities and relationships with others and the world at large. Their auxiliary function of Extraverted Intuition fosters a need for some sort of community setting, whether a small group or a large organization.

> *Sometimes I can be captivated by music or ritualistic ceremony when (and only when) I get past my initial suspicions and doubts about the authenticity of it all. If I listen to the words of a teaching or song, I am more likely to criticize it and resist it. I think that's why I prefer readings in Hebrew. It provides the meditation of chant. But when it is in English, I struggle to turn my mind from its debating mode.*
> —Anne, 65, fine artist

Within these settings, INTPs might seek to use Extraverted Intuition by engaging in any of the exercises listed in the Extraverted Intuition (page 97), with goals such as

- encouraging exploration of broad topics that search out various "truths," while acknowledging differing opinions;
- helping organizations and people become as effective as possible;
- using a cognitive yet determined style that is well grounded in logical principles;
- becoming actively involved in the world;
- exploring other traditions and generating new possibilities for soulwork.

All of these might help them bring clarity to their beliefs and breadth to their soulwork.

> *I didn't think I could afford the time to get away from all the problems swirling in my mind. Just when every fiber in my being said, "Don't go," a friend dragged me out to play racquetball. Being with others and playing a challenging game removed all the furies of my*

overwrought mind. Now I know that these activities are essential. Getting the motivation to do it, however, can take all my logical and intuitive resources. After I return I almost never know why I had such a struggle in the first place.
　　　　—Sophie, 49, judge

What Might Push INTPs Away from Their Spiritual Path

With their drive for truth, clarity, and unifying principles, INTPs can be lead to believe, based on several factors, that their spiritual walk is not worth their time and energy. Common themes we heard from the people we interviewed included

- being in the company of those who disregard the intellectual aspects of spirituality. They don't accept the "Just believe" attitude some devout people put forth. If others, especially the INTP's teachers or guides, fail to rationally analyze or critique their own beliefs, settle for less than truthful conclusions, or try to press their own beliefs onto an INTP (or even onto others for that matter), then INTPs may dismiss these teachers as spiritually incompetent.

- focusing on inconsequential, tangential, or minor facets of soul-work as subjects worthy of serious debate—wearing of hats, hair length, times of day for specific events, diets, and so forth.

In my study of comparative religions, I was amazed at the universality of symbols of faith such as the roles of food and ritual in building community or the regulations regarding who wears or does not wear specific kinds of headgear. Sometimes I am in awe, other times I want to ask what all of this has to do with the big questions of belief.
　　　　—Kathleen, 32, cognitive psychologist

- wanting to avoid public displays of feelings or emotions. Preferring calmness in self and others, INTPs dislike straying from a cool, dispassionate mind-set and therefore avoid sharing in public their deeply private thoughts or emotions.

- being aware of the expectation of many spiritual traditions that one must have a heartfelt or mystical experience in order to be "truly spiritual." The INTP cerebral approach, valid for them, is often viewed as invalid and not spiritual by others.

I like to hear how you define spirituality, mainly because my definition appears to be very different from the spiritual experiences of others. However, so often when I ask for clarification, I get the implication that I'm not spiritual, which hurts and confuses me.
—Patrick, 28, reporter

- knowing that spiritual people can over rely on the truism that some things are beyond our human comprehension. While INTPs agree, they might argue that such truisms are still worth thinking about, not buying into "Keep things simple and just accept it on faith."

Trusted spiritual advisors, friends, and family can help INTPs find an enriching spiritual path by

- realizing that questioning beliefs is not meant to be critical but that INTPs are open to being influenced,
- presenting well-reasoned and objective analyses of beliefs in a manner that shows an understanding of INTPs' point of view,
- understanding that INTPs have emotional reactions but that these are often deeply guarded,
- stating their insights and conclusions concisely, getting to the essence of the matter.

When Life Is Difficult

The fourth, or *inferior*, function for INTPs is Extraverted Feeling. With their emphasis on logical analysis, tapping into the Extraverted Feeling realm of interpersonal awareness, relationships, and values is a struggle.

In times of stress, the inferior function can erupt, changing the INTP's behavior into a caricature of ESFJs and ENFJs for whom Extraverted Feeling is the *dominant* function. For INTPs in times of stress, the following circumstances might trigger their inferior function:

- When their grief or that of others causes emotional outbursts. Because INTPs approach life in an impersonal and often detached way, such eruptions can cause them even further distress. When one INTP concluded that her principles had been violated, she blurted out with uncharacteristic feeling, "Religion is for the simple-minded! You all should grow up and do your own thinking." She was later embarrassed, but it was too late to retract her comment.

- When their commitments or workload interfere with their need for autonomy and independence. Because INTPs thrive best when they have psychological space, quiet environments, and ample time for reflection, even the day-to-day push of modern life can be contrary to their soulwork.
- When situations or people appear arbitrary or illogical. INTPs may grow despondent, defiant, or develop physical symptoms of stress.

> *There was a terrible battle going on in my spiritual community. I did not take sides, seeing truth in both viewpoints. I tried to keep the dialogue open and to be helpful, only to find that both sides considered me as the enemy! It was a lose-lose situation overall—and an emotional one at that.*
> —Pia, 60, architect

- When others fail to grasp their ideas and analysis of the situation, despite the INTP's careful efforts to communicate.

Often the worst times for INTPs are when their rational, analytical approach and their ability to find inconsistencies or flaws in others' reasoning are employed to no avail. Perhaps they overused their dominant function, Thinking, assuming that an outwardly cool and objective approach to life's ups and downs will answer all their issues or questions. Then everything about emotional people and illogical situations becomes too hard to handle. Their inferior function Feeling takes a dark cast.

> *When my wife decided she wanted a divorce, I was devastated. I guess I appeared my normal reserved and calm self, but inside I felt a lot of pain. Talking with a few close friends helped and I went to a counselor for awhile. The intense pain faded after about a year, but I never did really understand why our marriage failed—that was difficult for me. I still find myself analyzing what went wrong. However, I realize now that part of my struggle was losing the option to rework the relationship. I coped by rational analysis, but analyzing the past couldn't bring back the options.*
> —Randy, 31, computer programmer

In these situations, INTPs might be uncharacteristically preoccupied with minor inconsistencies and hypersensitive to perceived slights or to emotional expressions in others. They might also move inward, closing off contact with people who might help or with the outside world in general. When these symptoms appear, a totally different approach to soulwork often helps. INTPs might *purposefully* pursue Extraverted Feeling. Its *conscious use* requires the INTP to shut down what is usually easiest—Introverted Thinking—which may have gotten out of control. In doing so, the INTP can slow down to concentrate on their own values and feelings.

Ways to consciously engage the Feeling function include

- focusing on relationships, being aware of the needs of others, and discovering what is personally meaningful. Some INTPs find it easier to share life's major hurts with people they scarcely know (sometimes with a person seated next to them on a bus or airplane).

- completing a values clarification exercise, comparing those values with ones held by significant people in their lives, and factoring subjective criteria into decisions. For many INTPs, stress is often a critical coexistent of spiritual development. Great emotional upheaval can lead to enhanced spiritual awareness.

- being with people in purely social or recreational activities—group volleyball, team sports, participating in spectator or other personally enjoyable activities. Moving away from the life of the mind into more physical or relational activities can help them resolve issues in a fresh way.

In the chosen activity, the key is backing away from uncontrolled sensitivity and emotion and engaging in a process that makes them pay attention to the impact of spirituality on their relationships with others and with God. As one INTP put it,

> During my crisis period, I discovered that "God is Love" is a simple word definition; appropriately used, the words are interchangeable. There is a basic underlying fact being referred to—the phrase itself, like life, is meaningless. People experience a oneness under varying circumstances. Call it love and you have labeled it, not explained it. However, whatever love is, it is a fact. Invoking it and living with it more often produces a difference perceptible to others.
>
> At mid-life, I rebuilt an internal model and learned how to live more consciously with other people externally. "You are more at peace with yourself; it is no longer upsetting to have you around"—a direct quote from my mother.
> —Ali, 54, chemist

As an INTP, I am thankful for
>my skepticism, which for me is a tool for getting at truth,
>my love of wrestling with complex issues that challenge and exercise my intellect,
>my curiosity that propels my search for truth,
>my understanding of the principles that regulate the universe.

When life is difficult, I can find support by
>focusing on the big picture and looking for new possibilities,
>using others as a sounding board to clarify my values,
>assessing the impact of the situation on those around me.

To honor myself and my pathway to God, I can
>pursue and analyze those areas where I doubt;
>honor my need for precision, enlightenment, and wholeness;
>explore the ways my soulwork can benefit my relationships with others.

The Paths of Feeling Spirituality

So many gods, so many creeds—
So many paths that wind and wind,
When just the art of being kind
Is all the sad world needs.[1]
—Ella Wheeler Wilcox

Feeling types find satisfying soulwork through

- living the spiritual life through avenues for personal meaning;
- enjoying the heart-felt longings and emotions of the spiritual journey;
- appreciating the beauty of relationships with others and the Creator;
- seeing applications for defining personal values, finding meaning, and individual and community growth;
- learning through understanding the motivations, inspirations, and examples of others;
- working to discern what is important for themselves and their community;
- evaluating the impact of soulwork on the inner and outer life.

Preferred Extraverted Feeling Soulwork (Ch. 9: ESFJ and ENFJ)	Preferred Introverted Feeling Soulwork (Ch. 10: ISFP and INFP)
• Prayer or meditation with and for the needs of people and community	• Prayer or meditation through silent petitions for others and longings of one's own heart
• Soulwork through meaningful interpersonal relationships	• Soulwork through a personal relationship with God
• Structured spiritual life, a basis for their commitment to others	• Spontaneous spiritual life, as a result of their observations or insights
• Service through involvement with people, organizing to meet group needs	• Service through defining values systems, interpersonal ideals, and modeling integrity and compassion

Suggestions for Feeling Spirituality

1. Read a favorite written prayer or passage of scripture, imagining that these prayers are being said specifically for you. (John 17 or Colossians 1:9-12 are examples.) Reread the words slowly, perhaps rewriting them. What specifics in your own petitions might these words address? What is your response to God who cares for you in these ways? Consider journaling your feelings as you consider the promises in these prayers.

2. "The noble-minded dedicate themselves to the promotion of peace and the happiness of others—even those who injure them" (a Hindu teaching).[2] What are the values of this statement? How do you relate to the values found in this teaching? If you were to espouse the values expressed in this statement, what kinds of conflicts might arise? When and how could these values be ineffective for you or others?

3. As you read this prayer by St. Francis of Assisi, make it your own petition. To what situations does it apply in your life? On which aspect (faith, joy, understanding, and so forth) do you most want to concentrate now? How will you do that?

> *Lord, make me an instrument of your peace.*
> *Where there is hatred, let me sow love,*
> *Where their is injury, pardon;*
> *Where there is doubt, faith;*
> *Where there is despair, hope;*
> *Where there is darkness, light;*
> *Where there is sadness, joy.*
> *Divine Master, Grant that I may not so much seek*
> *To be consoled, as to console,*
> *To be understood, as to understand,*
> *To be loved, as to love,*
> *For it is in giving that we receive;*
> *It is in pardoning that we are pardoned;*
> *It is in dying that we are born to eternal life.*[3]

4. For the discipline of simplicity: Take a hard look at your possessions, activities, serving roles, and forms of soulwork.
   - Which feed your soul?
   - Which prevent you from experiencing the things you value more?
   - Which do you try to do so "perfectly" that they block your joy?
   - Which truly add to your spirituality?
5. For the discipline of celebration: In addition to birthdays, anniversaries, and holidays, take time to honor and enjoy important relationships. Make sure you tell others how they have encouraged you. Ponder how empty your life would be without specific people. Then find ways to celebrate and give thanks for these people. Find time to spend with them. Send a card. Write out a prayer specifically for them (and let them see it). Give a gift to charity in their name or otherwise honor them and their relationship to you.
6. Ask someone you trust to comment on your spirituality by offering concrete and specific examples. What do they see as your strengths as a spiritual person? How can your gifts be developed further? Rejoice in having these attributes and consider what forms of soulwork might use them.
7. What styles of music or specific songs speak to the longings of your heart? Record onto one tape or CD several inspiring songs that remind you of the joys of your spiritual walk.
8. What are the ways you can bring harmony to your interactions with people so that they will want to know the specifics of your soulwork or perhaps strive to model themselves after you? Pause often to reflect on the ways in which you have been able to love your neighbor as yourself. Where can you add courtesy and kindness to the processes of your workplace, home, or spiritual community? Give thanks for the moments when you were open to others' needs.
9. Reflect on your past relationships. How have they aided your soulwork? Where have they hindered your spirituality? What key learning have you obtained in these relationships?

10. By declaring yourself a spiritual person, you may place yourself in situations of conflict. Clarify the values you wish to see reflected in your life.
    - How does your spirituality support your values or the way you live your life?
    - What value conflicts do you expect because of your spirituality?
    - How can your being open to those conflicts inform and enrich your spirituality?

    Ponder or journal on the changes you want to make to bring your life more into line with your values.

Extraverted Feeling Soulwork

1. Make two lists: the things you *have* to do for other people and the things you do for others that bring you *joy*. If your first list is too long, put a star by those tasks that someone else could do, a check by those that you feel inadequate in handling, and a diamond by those where you struggle to love the people you serve. What patterns arise? Is your life in balance? Evaluate all these tasks to see how they fit with your personal values and needs. What changes could be made? Then, find time for self care: reaffirm your gifts, allow yourself to exercise and eat healthfully, take a nap—and affirm for yourself that this is indeed soulwork. Notice the energy you have for your mind and your body as you work to be a better steward of *yourself.* Remember at times to allow others the chance to serve you.

2. For the discipline of study: Reflect on your interpersonal relationships and those of others. Look to the facts, meanings, and truths, but devote the majority of your study time to the impact and implications of those relationships. What are the values and motivations of each individual? What controls them? What helps them? What lessons are there for your life?

3. For the discipline of prayer: As you meditate or pray about your own needs or those of others, listen for ideas of what you might be able to do for them. Are you being called to serve beyond the very real need for prayer? If so, record your ideas and actions. Then at a

later time, look back on how you and others benefited from your prayers or actions.

4. Form or join a small group for regular prayer, study, worship, or other regular pursuit of soulwork. Seek those who would also like some structure—books with questions for small groups or a formal Bible study. In one such group, each member keeps a notebook with everyone's prayer requests. In another, they meet at the same time each week but in different homes, rotating who chooses their study materials. Add food and fellowship for soulwork you won't want to miss.

Introverted Feeling Soulwork

1. Nurture a special relationship for the purpose of mutual spiritual growth. You might meet regularly, correspond, study together, share difficulties and joys, or simply hold each other accountable for meeting spiritual goals.

2. For the discipline of prayer: Make a notebook for prayer by collecting poems, sacred readings, or meaningful quotes. Offer them as prayers, either for yourself or for others. Examples might be:

And this is my prayer, that your love may overflow more and more with knowledge and full insight to help you to determine what is best, so that in the day of Christ you may be pure and blameless (Philippians 1:9-10).

Let me not wander in vain.
Let me not labor in vain.
Let me not mingle with the prejudiced.
Let me not leave the company of the virtuous.
Let me not fly into anger.
Let me not stray off the path of goodness.
Let me not seek for this day or for the morrow.
Give me such a wealth, O Almighty![4]
　　—Pattinatar, 10th century

3. For the discipline of study: Consider learning from inspiring literature, films, biographies, or magazines as legitimate soulwork. Choose titles with admirable characters and compare their motivations, struggles, and triumphs with your own. How can you apply the authors' messages to your own life?

4. Ponder the fact that you are created and of value just as you are. What does this imply for your life? What about the lives of others? How is that value encouraged, supported, or nourished?

CHAPTER NINE

EXTRAVERTED FEELING:

The Community-Oriented Spiritual Path

Exraverted Feeling Spirituality
ESFJ, ENFJ

Living a spiritual life filled with personal meaning.
Applying faith and values in leading and helping others.
Knowing what matters by understanding the motivations,
inspirations, and examples of others.

O ur experiences with Extraverted Feeling types were the exact opposite of our e-mail communications from Introverted Thinking types. The Extraverted Feelers invited us to their homes for coffee and conversation. At one *SoulTypes* seminar, the Extraverted Feelers wrote the following definition of spirituality on their flip chart paper:

It's All about People

Indeed, Extraverted Feeling spirituality is about meaningful relationships with God and with others. Soulwork becomes an authentic way to bring love and caring to the world. Their spiritual path is more relationship-centered than theological as they strive to help people value themselves and others.

> *I enjoy seeing people grow and develop to be all they can be. I believe that I'm doing God's work when I am contributing to this nurturing of people's uniqueness and individuality. The activities that attract me most are those that encourage others to see themselves as God sees them—worthy of love and approval. If more people received affirmation for who they are, everyone's life would be so much better.*
> —Sally, 58, psychotherapist

With their natural desire to reach out to others, Extraverted Feeling types are drawn to the concept of a Creator who provides support, encouragement, and strength, no matter what life brings. Fostering acceptance, cooperation, and harmony are often important values. Often their most meaningful soulwork comes through striving to make the world a better place.

With this understanding, spirituality becomes a steadfast rudder in times of need. Extraverted Feeling types volunteer, lead, and assist with efforts that have educational, benevolent, or spiritual purposes. Often, they contribute energy and enthusiasm to such a degree that others may find it hard-going without them.

> *Some people misunderstand my soulwork because it takes place outside of organized religion. There's a simple reason: Any time I join a spiritual community, I end up in charge of something! I have to pick and choose where I put my energy to work and right now I believe I can do more good with people who have no relationship with a God or Higher Power.*
>
> *I am a deeply spiritual person—my soulwork is what I do as I seek to help other people through my volunteer work. I've found joy in it all, from organizing fundraising drives to sitting with a child who flew from halfway around the world to have heart surgery. Life is about helping others and making a difference. I can't abide people who think of themselves first. I work to make my organization serve people, not process them.*
> —Juanita, 49, hospice administrator

Extraverted Feeling types focus on what is positive in spiritual pathways, leaders, and sacred texts and note what is worthy of appreciation. They invite others to join them in this process. Many religious and spiritual leaders are from the ranks of the Extraverted Feeling types.

Prayer

Prayer for Extraverted Feeling types often involves acts of service for others as well as prayers with and for the needs of people and community. Prayer has a personal side to it, based on the value of acting out one's faith in the larger world.

- Extraverted Feeling types scan the environment and where they find needs they offer prayer, along with rolling up their sleeves to help. They pray as they act to meet the needs of people and community.
- Many Extraverted Feeling types engage in meaningful, regular disciplines for prayer. They might use a book of prayer or methods they learn through reading, taking classes, or talking with friends about what works for them. However, their prayer is rarely formal or routine; indeed, it needs to be warm, personal, and congruent with their current state of being. Nothing is withheld from God as Extraverted Feeling types see prayer as a conversation, a good exchange of ideas and realities, with God.
- The prayer of Extraverted Feeling types aims to stir the heart and to get people into action. Some experience "peak experiences" in their prayers as their relationship with God and their desire to serve stir their emotions.
- Some Extraverted Feeling types involve their whole selves in their prayer by using such modalities as healing touch. Their entire being becomes a sounding board for the wants and needs of others and themselves.

Worship

Many Extraverted Feeling types participate regularly in worship; they develop friendships and enjoy the communal aspect that worship affords.

- Worship may serve as a bridge among generations, a way to feel connected with others and with the past.

I attend morning prayers at our spiritual community as often as I can. Some of my friends wonder why it doesn't get tiresome for me. Along with the ritual that feeds my soul, I know I'm dedicating a portion of my day to my faith and participating the same ritual as many generations of women.
    —Elaine, 67, retired

- Extraverted Feeling types want their worship to bring about congruence between ideals and action, both personally and for groups or communities. They often seek communities that welcome everyone, yet are tolerant of paradox—even seeking paradox as a gateway to growth.
- Many Extraverted Feeling types enjoy designing their own and others' worship experiences. "I love to come up with ways that we can worship that are different yet still as spiritual as the ones we might experience in formal worship," said one Extraverted Feeling type.

When I am part of a passive group, my mind tends to brainstorm ways to improve things. I came up with several suggestions to make our community gatherings more appealing for both the young families and older members who attend. However, the leadership did not allow people to express their ideas, nor did they attempt to be flexible. I finally quit attending as the complaints of those around me increased. Now I lead a small study group that really appreciates my efforts and preparations.
    —Florian, 52, actor

Study

Extraverted Feeling types enjoy reading and studying about other people and their spiritual walks, thereby finding inspiration for their own lives.

- Most Extraverted Feeling types enjoy the social aspect of learning and, therefore, many of their study practices involve being with others who want to learn. They might participate in retreats, study or support groups, classes, or seminars that involve both interaction with others and time for introspection. Many also enjoy taking a leadership role in these endeavors, putting to work their ability to discern what others need.

Our community saw a huge increase in people in the midst of job transition. When I conveyed to the staff at my spiritual community how people in job transition might benefit from a support group, they provided the financial resources and space for me to launch the program.
—Renaldo, 28, middle manager

- They also benefit from dialoguing with others about their spiritual journeys—how they reached decisions about specific or global spiritual issues and how their faith supported them. The personal experiences of people they know or care about provide them with insights and motivation to do their own spiritual study and decision-making.

- Extraverted Feeling types also study the lives of others as models for their spiritual path. They work to define spiritual concepts and values from their own personal experience and that of people they admire, to learn what each means for their soulwork.

Service

With their ideals of mercy and justice, Extraverted Feeling types often take on leadership roles to put their faith into action. Service to the world and individuals in need is key to their spirituality. They work to hold individuals and organizations accountable for making actions congruent with ideals.

- Many take leadership roles in organizing events, educating children and adults, or greeting and hosting people in ways that help them feel welcomed and appreciated.

- Extraverted Feeling types typically make others feel included and welcomed by their warm and friendly demeanor. In many cases they are the social glue that holds together the fabric of their spiritual communities.

- Working together in groups to bring the good and necessary things to the lives of others (for example, clothing drives, medical help, tutoring) helps Extraverted Feeling types live up to their values and grow spiritually.

I gladly took on rearranging and stocking the children's resource room at our place of worship. I knew that my approach would make it easier for volunteers to quickly find what they needed—and I even provided things they didn't yet know they'd need! Having everything

in its place makes it much easier for the volunteers and makes people more willing to give of their time.
    —Renee, 26, teacher

Other Forms of Soulwork

For most Extraverted Feeling types, soulwork is a vehicle to bring about congenial and empathetic relationships to make the world a better place.

- Extraverted Feeling types look for groups where they can safely share their hopes and concerns with others. They enjoy hearing the basis for others' life choices, ways God acted in their lives, and stories of faith in action.

    For me, building relationships with people is the most important purpose in life. I can easily nurture my soul by gathering with others who share my values and beliefs, especially when we've had the chance to connect on a personal level and gain a sense of shared history. I appreciate the encouragement of others who think that our efforts can make things better for humankind. That may sound overly altruistic to some people, but my spirituality and sense of hope are intertwined.
    —Lara, 40, teacher

- Soulwork also takes the form of helping others in their search for wholeness. They work with people to ensure their well-being in ways that maximize human potential.
- Extraverted Feeling types' most spiritual moments often come as they experience emotional healing, or even well-being, in themselves or in others.

    At one time, I needed others to be strong for me, providing guidance for my choices. I thought other people were more capable than I was, so I relinquished some responsibility for myself. Then I joined a book club in my neighborhood. Even though we discussed secular novels, the themes gave us a chance to share at a deep, spiritual level. As I met with these other women regularly to discuss fictional heroines, I was encouraged by their examples to explore my own talents. I found that I have leadership abilities, I'm gifted at organizing events, and everyone seems to feel at home when I arrange things. Looking back, I was like an ostrich with its head in the sand, hiding from the

unknown when I had all the capabilities to deal with it and didn't know it.
    —Kristell, 29, office manager

In short, Extraverted Feeling helps us all remember that

- acting on our values and honoring those of others is a loving thing to do, especially for those closest to you,
- joining with others in community allows us to accomplish tasks that are too much for any one individual,
- reaching out and communicating the warmth and affection felt for others spreads joy,
- focusing on what is positive in spiritual pathways, leaders, and sacred texts and noting what is worthy of gratitude and appreciation moves all of us into a more generous spirituality.

The Second Half of Life's Spiritual Journey

While Extraverted Feeling is about living out one's values and being in community, life grows short. As do all personalities, the Extraverted Feeling types begin to wonder whether they have found sufficient meaning and purpose. Have they chosen the best path?

Often at this stage, the Extraverted Feeling types have developed their natural spiritual path. Then, richness comes through the inferior function, Introverted Thinking. This involves

- choosing one's spiritual path through an objective process of examination,
- raising doubts to bring clarity to an issue,
- searching for universal principles,
- defining categories and standards to apply to spiritual issues.

While Extraverted Feeling types may continue many of their favorite methods of soulwork, here are some examples of what they found as they journeyed on into Introverted Thinking.

The prove/disprove approach to theology now fascinates me, whereas I once found it irrelevant to the "real" purpose of faith—building relationships. Now I can better reach out to others because my beliefs are more grounded.

I'm more inclined to want an academic approach to spiritual learning experiences. Before, I wanted to know how the sacred texts applied to my life and relationships. Now I'm just as interested in alternative explanations for the origins of certain stories and their cultural context. Understanding these things allows me to better explain them to others.

I've done a lot of work around my need for harmony. Sometimes it simply isn't logical for people to agree. With this truth now firmly ingrained, I can embrace the fact that disagreement is sometimes healthy and can even be a starting point for transformation. I'm much freer to concentrate on the issue at hand than the squabbling among the people around me.

After identifying specific examples of how I have experienced each concept, I defined for myself what words such as love, truth, and wisdom meant. I looked at how these concepts were used in different contexts, how they applied to different areas of my life, and made the new meanings part of my experience.

I realized that as I was approaching 60 I had a tad less energy than I did as a 40-year-old. I've always had a full calendar and I love being with people, but now I need some time to do just what I want—even to be alone. In order to get that time, I took out my yearly schedule and listed all of my commitments. I then assigned a higher numeric value to those things that met three conditions: no one else could do them, they gave me the greatest joy, and they allowed me to learn. By using a logical analysis for elimination, I found some time in my schedule just for me.

Any of the Introverted Thinking pathways (chapter 8) can bring this kind of rest and richness if Extraverted Feeling types allow their dominant functions a time of rest and let the Spirit guide their thoughts and actions.

ESFJ

Extraverted Sensing
Feeling Judging

Spirituality in the outer world of people and experiences

For I am not seeking my own good but the good of many, so that they may be saved.
—*1 Corinthians 10:33*

Greatest Gifts

A deliberate yet compassionate approach to life; Adeptness in interpersonal endeavors; Discerning the specific needs of self and others; Radiating warmth and friendship

Role in Community

Making people feel welcome and valued by understanding what matters for the welfare of the community; Emphasizing cooperation and tolerance in serving others

---

ESFJs tend to be organized, structured, and responsible in achieving their goals for meeting day-to-day needs. They are reliable, straightforward, outgoing types who enjoy managing others, working harmoniously to complete tasks in a timely fashion. ESFJs are typically tactful, caring leaders who focus on building good relationships.

Using their dominant function, Extraverted Feeling, is the natural starting place for soulwork. However, their auxiliary or second function,

Introverted Sensing, calls them to quiet moments so they can review their experiences and look at current reality, then determine their view of circumstances based on this practical information.

Soulwork through the Second Function

ESFJs can use reflection time to inform their decision-making by asking what the facts reveal and finding the basis for their value judgments. What does their common sense say about their situation? Introverted Sensing can also help them to take better care of themselves.

> *To outsiders who are used to my normal bubbly self, my withdrawal might seem almost depression-like. However, I simply get to a point of overcommitment where I realize I'm not doing anyone any good. I take stock of my own needs and indulge in some restoring activities—hot tub soaks, my favorite foods, catering to my own tastes for a time. Then I feel recharged and am able to turn outward again.*
> —Aliza, 52, full-time volunteer

Many ESFJs report they like this different avenue for soulwork, taking delight in spiritual discovery by using their five senses. Candles, incense, music, devotions, or pictures often aid the ESFJs' spiritual practice. Detail-oriented projects that require precision may also allow them to ponder the present, such as cross-stitch, model-building, automotive work, or even balancing the checkbook.

> *I see the variety of fish in the zoo aquarium and take note of all the different colors, designs, and textures of the marine life. God created all of this—no combination of random forces could have produced such delightful results.*
> —Jessa, 41, support group facilitator

ESFJs can also engage their Introverted Sensing function by structuring time for reflective spiritual disciplines. They may choose to engage in time-honored practices such as following the suggestions in a book of prayer or designing a personal ritual that they use regularly, appreciating the richness of traditions, noticing and remembering both internal and external details and applying soulwork to practical, personal needs.

Within these settings, ESFJs might seek to use Introverted Sensing by engaging in any of the exercises listed in the Sensing section (pages 49-52), with goals such as

- engaging in reflective spiritual disciplines for depth and ease of understanding;
- reviewing past experiences for their spiritual significance;
- delighting in the five senses—what can be seen, heard, touched, smelled, or tasted—to enrich spirituality;
- applying soulwork to practical, personal needs;
- reassessing the facts and realities of the situations they face to inform their decisions.

All of these might help them bring clarity to their beliefs and depth to their soulwork.

What Might Push ESFJs Away from Their Spiritual Path

Most ESFJs enjoy their early church experiences, chalking up perfect attendance records, developing friendships, and enjoying traditions. However, if harmony, warmth, and acceptance are absent, their desire for soulwork can be hampered or closed down entirely. Common themes we heard from the ESFJs we interviewed included

- having a spiritual concept of shame or one of God as judge. ESFJs set high standards for themselves and may fall into the trap of thinking, "God has a yardstick and no matter how hard I try, I can't measure up." They also set high standards for others and become disappointed when people act all too human.
- experiencing a form of spirituality that is based on manipulation and emotional appeals. ESFJs can be vulnerable to such tactics themselves as they search for concrete evidence of love—either from God or from other people in a spiritual community. However, once "burned," ESFJs are often superior judges of manipulation and artifice, especially as it relates to the emotional domain, and can quickly spot this kind of fakery.

  I've learned by experience what to look for and what's genuine. Now I'm a pretty strong barometer for others and myself whenever there is manipulation or game playing. I can point out and label it for what it truly is—an attempt to win a point by using emotional subterfuge.
  —Griffin, 45, pediatrician

- desiring to promote harmony so much that it keeps them from acknowledging when conflict or disagreements are actually happening. Externally, ESFJs may proceed as if nothing has occurred. However, inside, deep hurt may reside and ESFJs may sit on their feelings, thinking, "I shouldn't feel that way." The eventual awareness of the conflict or that people have been hurt can cause ESFJs to feel doubt, grief, or anger. These circumstances can lead even the most devout to experience a crisis of faith.

I took a leadership role in a volunteer recruitment effort because I so believed in its purpose. However, things went wrong and my hopes for harmony were dashed by constant bickering and second-guessing. Now I realized how I stuffed it—I should have spoken up at the first hint from my inner feeling that certain people were acting in ways that would defeat everyone's efforts.
—Ted, 33, retail manager

- sticking with one religious or spiritual tradition out of loyalty and possibly not examining other, perhaps more appealing, faiths. ESFJs may overlook the faults in their own traditions and not be constructively critical when necessary until they either reach spiritual maturity or their discomfort is too huge to deny.

Trusted spiritual advisors, friends, and family can help ESFJs find an enriching spiritual path by

- talking through spiritual issues and explaining the basis for their life choices as models for ESFJs to consider;
- contributing their fair share and assuming some responsibility so that ESFJs don't feel overburdened;
- showing their love in concrete ways, especially when ESFJs feel undeserving or are in the midst of a crisis;
- helping ESFJs remember to have faith when they feel concerned about the welfare of people they love.

When Life Is Difficult

The fourth, or *inferior*, function for ESFJs is Introverted Thinking. With their focus on understanding people, living in step with their values, and serving others in practical ways, ESFJs can struggle to tap into the Introverted Thinking realm of critical analysis and logical examination of the spiritual journey.

In times of stress, the inferior function can erupt, changing the ESFJ's behavior into a caricature of INTPs and ISTPs for whom Introverted

Thinking is the *dominant* function. For ESFJs in times of stress, the following circumstances might trigger the inferior function:

- When they are asked to compromise their values.
- When the storm results in conflict and when ESFJs feel responsible or blamed, especially by people close to them. If major disagreements erupt over decisions that must be made, if values are compromised, or if interpersonal niceties are completely tossed aside, ESFJs may become discouraged, disappointed, and stressed.
- When they are not supported emotionally. With all the help they give to others, when ESFJs themselves need to be encouraged, nourished, or cared for and that support is not forthcoming or is presented in an unsuitable way ESFJs may feel slighted or, at the worst, deserted.
- When their careful efforts to organize structures or events fail to prevent others from being hurt. ESFJs may experience feelings of guilt, betrayal, or deep injustice in these extreme situations.

> *Even though I couldn't help the people involved, I felt I should have been able to ward off the problem. I was so upset with myself that I refused every offer of help from friends and family. I shoved away the support when I needed it the most.*
> —Victor, 37, nurse

Often the worst times for ESFJs are when they try to keep everyone happy and everything organized, reach out to others, and perform all of their usual and many roles. Perhaps they have overused their dominant function, Extraverted Feeling, and are using up their reserves by not listening to their souls crying for rest. Then it may take a major insight or new information before they can again focus on what is truly important to them. In the worst times, a totally different approach to soulwork may be the only refuge.

> *With the perspective of the passing of time, I realize how my lack of self-confidence made me vulnerable to an unhealthy relationship. For three years I tried everything to please my boyfriend. I guess I had a wacky sense of loyalty and follow-through. Then one morning after we'd had a terrible fight, I realized that I was actually frightened of him. I started listing out the details of our relationship. The good times and beneficial facts did not outweigh the problems. For the first time,*

I thought about making this person the father of my children—and immediately walked to a pay phone to call my own parents. It took me a long time to sort out my feelings and define for myself what I needed in a relationship, but I made the effort to do so.
—Kendall, 29, X-ray technician

In these situations, ESFJs might be excessively critical of themselves and others, withdrawing from group activities and camaraderie. Some ESFJs may overanalyze problems—consulting too many "experts," or reading too many "expert" sources. When these symptoms appear, a totally different approach to soulwork often helps. ESFJs might *purposefully* pursue Introverted Thinking. Its *conscious use* requires ESFJs to shut down what is usually easiest—Extraverted Feeling—which may have gotten out of control. By doing so, ESFJs can slow down and practice good self-care (eating properly, resting, and exercising), perhaps start a project that's fun, or make a needed change in their routine.

Ways to consciously engage the Introverted Thinking function include

- talking through the situation with an impartial third party. Since logic is not a strong suit for ESFJs, hearing someone else's views of the pros and cons or the causes and implications of their actions often brings about new solutions to problems.

- analyzing books, movies, or the experiences of other people. Some ESFJs consciously consider the points of view and motivations of several fictional characters or friends and then try to determine the logic these people used. In departing from their appreciative style, ESFJs may come to new understandings to augment their people-oriented experiences.

- working puzzles or playing games that engage the mind in more intellectual ways can help to refresh ESFJs.

In the chosen activity, the key is backing away from uncontrolled analysis or criticality and engaging in a process that makes the enjoyment of people possible again. As one ESFJ put it, "I try to remember that crabbiness for me is a signal to remember God's presence and gifts to me—and to slow down. I call a friend for lunch, drive the long way home in order to rethink my priorities, and take time for reflection until my normal, appreciative perspective returns."

As an ESFJ, I am thankful for

my ability to befriend and care for people,

my warm and enthusiastic manner,

being in tune with feelings of others and knowing what is important in life,

the way I invite others in so we can all join in serving the common good.

When life is difficult, I can find support by

finding space and quiet time to reflect on the facts of the situation;

realizing my personal limitations and what is beyond my control;

assessing what I value, what is most important for my own life, before choosing to serve.

To honor myself and my pathway to God, I can

develop a few intimate "spiritual friendships" that allow for deep conversations and examination;

celebrate myself, others, and the beauty in the universe as expressions of the Divine;

explore what my logical mind can add to my heartfelt soulwork.

ENFJ

Extraverted Intuition
Feeling Judging

*Spirituality in the outer world of
possibilities for people*

*"For I know the plans I have for you," says the Lord, "plans to prosper you
and not to harm you, plans to give you hope and a future."*
—Jeremiah 29:11

Greatest Gifts

Seeing the positive in people and situations as well as the possibilities
for improvement; Articulating their own needs and the desires of others,
helping them grow into wholeness

Role in Community

Generating enthusiasm and building camaraderie; Communicating
with zest and commitment; Motivating and leading people and organizations toward the community's mission and core values

ENFJs tend to be lively and friendly communicators who seek to
inspire others to work together toward the development of people or the
institutions that serve them. Warm, interpersonally aware, caring, and
cooperative, ENFJs listen to aspirations and then create, organize, and
structure processes to meet them.

Using their dominant function, Extraverted Feeling, is the natural
starting place for soulwork. However, their auxiliary or second function,

Introverted Intuition, calls them to pull back from their active lifestyle for reflection.

Soulwork through the Second Function

Reflective space and time alone allows ENFJs to focus on their soulwork—on ideas and aspirations for themselves, others, and causes they hold dear. Introverted Intuition helps ENFJs generate numerous possibilities or options that give new insights on the issues or interactions they face.

Some ENFJs use solitude, perhaps journaling or meditating, to gain a different perspective on how a given situation affected them and what additional interpretations might be made of what actually occurred.

Using both their gifts of Extraverted Feeling and Introverted Intuition allows many ENFJs to move toward *whole* personhood—in keeping with their spiritual path of personal growth and development. Even a few hours alone, retreating from their external obligations, allows them a mental space to come up with new insights and possibilities.

> *I use my intuition to find patterns and deeper meanings in the spiritual books I read. These patterns help me understand what is happening in my own life—I especially find helpful those connections I glean when I'm reading about others who've come up against and then surmounted similar obstacles. However, to do this, I have to quiet down, allowing myself plenty of uninterrupted time for the nuances to flow.*
> —Ian, 24, artist

Within these settings, ENFJs might seek to use Introverted Intuition by engaging in any of the exercises listed in the Intuition section (pages 94-98), with goals such as

- generating new possibilities for people;
- focusing on insights and aspirations for themselves, others, and causes they hold dear;
- reflecting on future possibilities that are imaginative and broad in scope;
- concentrating on what is unseen, inexplicable, and mystical about spirituality;
- looking at life's events with a sense of the reality of the impossible that involves purposes bigger than we can comprehend.

All of these might help them bring clarity to their beliefs and depth to their soulwork.

> *Being with God in a silent, connecting way leads me to my own thoughts. These often help me deepen my faith and add to my awareness of myself, other people, and my spiritual journey. While I prefer to pray with others, praying alone, perhaps while walking, can help me discover new ideas.*
> —Jennifer, 41, minister

What Might Push ENFJs Away from Their Spiritual Path

With their quest for personal growth and development for themselves and others, many ENFJs find a spiritual path to be most inviting. However, if values are violated or contention exists, their instinctive desire to connect with others can shut down. Common themes we heard from the ENFJs we interviewed included

- being in atmospheres that are devoid of harmony or that are at odds with their values system. ENFJs whose personal relationships are negative may struggle to find meaningful paths for soulwork. In addition, problems within spiritual communities can be problematic for them if they see no way to change the interpersonal dynamics.

> *I put my whole heart into my commitments or else I wouldn't be involved in such a dedicated way. I also strive for warm and pleasing relationships with others. When I've given of myself that way, I expect to stay unless the person or organization crosses one of my deeply held values or beliefs. Then, well, I can really turn a cold shoulder.*
> —Wendy, 35, family practice physician

- being overcommitted—taking the weight of the world on their shoulders then experiencing a lack of appreciation for their efforts. Burnout can result for ENFJs, especially when they are so committed that they take little time for rejuvenation.
- struggling with a spiritual concept of shame or of God as judge. The standards that ENFJs set for soulwork and their responsibilities toward other people may be so high that they feel like they continually fall short, leading to their discouragement.
- losing patience when spiritual traditions become too bureaucratic and people are overlooked in the process. ENFJs may become

frustrated if they lack opportunities to influence their spiritual communities to avoid these problems. They may take a public stand or go elsewhere if they perceive that the needs of some people are being ignored.

Trusted spiritual advisors, friends, and family can help ENFJs find an enriching spiritual path by

- encouraging them to consider themselves and their own needs and wants;
- gently confronting them, especially when they insist on everyone getting along, and reminding them that the best of relationships can grow as a result of conflict;
- giving them permission to develop imaginative and creative ways for people to grow both personally and spiritually;
- providing a personal and caring environment for them. When there is heavy criticism or judgment, ENFJs may wither and want to offer less to others.

When Life Is Difficult

The fourth, or *inferior*, function for ENFJs is Introverted Thinking. With their emphasis on seeing the worth and dignity in all people, themselves included, and their natural appreciation of others and of the world at large, tapping into the Introverted Thinking realm of critical and objective thinking can be difficult.

In times of stress, the inferior function can erupt, changing the ENFJ's behavior into a caricature ISTPs and INTPs for whom Introverted Thinking is the *dominant* function. For ENFJs in times of stress, the following circumstances might trigger their inferior function:

- When their core values are violated. ENFJs seek congruency between expressed and acted-upon ideals and are deeply shaken when their important beliefs are compromised, misapplied, or ignored.
- When ENFJs perceive a problem as their fault. Stress often results for them and may bring about a strong bodily reaction.

I noticed I developed hives just about the time our missions team started to fight over which project would be funded first. I was not expecting the intensity of conviction so many team members had for

*very different projects. It was a painful experience both emotionally—
and as I now see—physically, too!*
—Andrew, 55, nonprofit executive

- When a situation is contentious.
- When ENFJs or those they care about are belittled, misunderstood, or patronized. They can feel angry or despondent. Because ENFJs see human relationships as *the* most important aspect of life and because their values set often includes a sense of meeting people at least halfway, ENFJs can be particularly upset when relationships have a competitive up-down, in-out, or me-versus-you manner.

Often the worst of times for ENFJs are when they focus too intently on restoring cooperation and harmony, sometimes to the point of enmeshment. ENFJs tend to worry about receiving the disapproval of people they admire or even of God. They may therefore hold back from contributing their own special ideas. Thus, their aversion to conflict sometimes robs them of working to change patterns in themselves or others, or intervening in situations and adding their own valid point of view.

> *I had worked so hard to understand the positions of each of the members of my committee that I was shocked when two of them accused me of self-serving motives in planning our next gathering. My every word, my every action, had been for the reconciliation of everyone. That night as I talked the situation over with my spouse, I even considered resigning as chair rather than cause any more disharmony. Fortunately, my spouse provided a more objective view of what had happened.*
> —Norika, 27, office assistant

In these situations, ENFJs might uncharacteristically exhibit hostility to others or try too hard to "make" people get along; they may avoid customary interests or become sidetracked by poor logic. When these symptoms appear, a totally different approach to soulwork often helps. ENFJs might *purposefully* pursue Introverted Thinking. Its *conscious use* requires ENFJs to shut down what is usually easiest—Extraverted Feeling—which may have gotten out of control. By doing so, ENFJs can slow down to set aside some roles and responsibilities in order to find time for reflection, rest, and a reordering of their priorities. They may also make a change in their routine to have time for self-care.

Ways to consciously engage the Thinking function include

- talking through the situation with an impartial third party. Since logic is not a strong suit for ENFJs, hearing someone else's views of their actions often brings enlightenment and calm.
- doing a pro and con analysis of each current responsibility, then gathering input from someone who cares. Using this exercise to clarify which tasks are too taxing, no longer necessary, or better done by others helps ENFJs reduce overload.
- playing strategy-oriented board games or ones that involve mysteries. ENFJs often find that such activities allow them to be with friends without having to discuss and deal with the problems they are facing. Other ENFJs complete crossword puzzles or cryptograms to reduce stress.

In the chosen activity, the key is allowing the emotions to rest, taking a greater interest in the world of the mind as well as the world of the heart. As one ENFJ put it, "By completing a logical analysis of my activities, I eliminated some and found time in my schedule for myself and my spiritual walk."

As an ENFJ, I am thankful for

my understanding of what matters most;

my friendly, warm, people-centered style;

my gifts of communication and creativity that allow me to advance human aspirations;

my passion for helping others become whole.

When life is difficult, I can find support by

pulling inward and considering all the hopeful possibilities;

assessing what is most important and finding personal confirmation for my values system;

being direct with others about my views, letting them know where I stand.

To honor myself and my pathway to God, I can

gather with kindred spirits for inspiration and understanding;

champion efforts to create the atmospheres for nurturing human potential I can so clearly envision;

determine the logical underpinnings of my values and beliefs in order to confirm what my heart already knows.

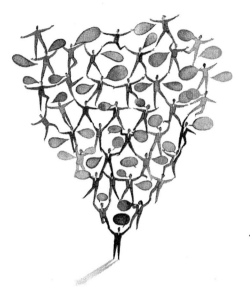

CHAPTER TEN

INTROVERTED FEELING:

The Personal Spiritual Path

Introverted Feeling Spirituality
ISFP, INFP

*An intensely personal spiritual path using beliefs
to form foundational values to guide life events
and tailoring individual soulwork around what is important.*

Deep within the heart and soul resides the essence of Introverted Feeling spirituality. Often Introverted Feeling types struggle to give voice to their ideals, values, or faith. Our best sources for *SoulTypes* were close, close friends and relatives. One told us, "I can't put into words what God means to me. What comes out sounds either childish or flat—and my relationship with God is anything but that. So I choose not to say anything rather than fall short of the way I feel."

Introverted Feeling spirituality is an ongoing journey and a private one at that. They often find the spiritual close at hand in the actions of others and the details of life. When Introverted Feeling types reach a level of inner certainty in their belief system they welcome discussions with others, but usually not before—their beliefs are too precious to them, serving as a foundation for the values that guide their lives.

Service to others is also a hallmark of the spirituality of Introverted Feeling types—often service behind the scenes—that matches their values with the needs they see. They often influence others to respond through their own examples of integrity, loyalty, inspiration, and support.

> *For me, spirituality is a force that helps me serve others. If the religions of the world didn't at least point us in the direction of goodness, there'd be a lot more suffering and chaos. I can put up with the weaknesses of organized religion because I wonder if the world would even have survived this long without it!*
> —Val, 45, office manager

Many Introverted Feeling types delight in the mysteries of spirituality and some of them are among the most open of all to mysticism—unseen and synchronistic experiences that make up the fabric of everyday life. Others find faith in the spontaneous gifts that the world of the senses provides.

> *One of my close friends is, in my mind, an ideal, joyful servant to other people. When I learned that she found inspiration in her spirituality to live out her values and beliefs, I became more interested in my own soulwork. Her particular religious community, where I frequently attend, encourages open discussion of issues for which there are no easy answers. It's large enough that I can choose my activities but stay anonymous when I so desire. There are many avenues for me to quietly act on what I believe. I think God is about helping the walking wounded of the world, not creating more of them through insensitivity and judgmentalism.*
> —Britte, 36, small-business owner

Introverted Feeling spirituality is also about tapping into one's spiritual nature while tending a garden, caring for pets or children, or being in the midst of favorite solitary activities. The beauty in the world and their own ability to nurture other living things reminds Introverted Feeling types of their Creator and helps them listen to their souls.

For most Introverted Feeling types, personal relationships are an important part of their spirituality, either with people or with God.

Soulwork provides them with a link to others and to important purposes of life. With their concern for living out their ideals, they are often alert for hypocrisy, judgmental comments, and intolerance on the part of organized spiritual communities or "pious individuals."

> *I welcome diversity of belief and tradition and feel a tie to anyone who is open to soulwork. No one issue is too big or, for that matter, too small to address. I enjoy the dialogue differences create. I'm sure that God knows there's diversity in the ways and means of faith. To me, spirituality is definitely not a "one size fits all" proposition.*
> —Pavel, 44, psychologist

Prayer

Prayer for Introverted Feeling types often involves examining the sentiments of one's own heart as well as offering petitions for others. Introverted Feelers have produced some of the greatest teachings in many of the world's spiritual traditions on meditation, prayer, and other spiritual disciplines—in some circles, their methods are the *only* ones taught.

- Introverted Feeling types usually find that their prayer includes a sense of intimacy where they talk with God about their ideas, their day's activities, or their relationships, including their relationship to God.
- Being able to find the good in people, leaders, spiritual communities, and nature becomes a part of their prayer, which also includes requests for support and comfort. Their prayers deal more directly with the affective or "feeling" aspects of life. Emotions are a key part of Feeling prayer—the good and the bad, the happy and the angry.
- Introverted Feeling types are drawn to pray through journaling, meditation, reflection on values, or simply spending time in favorite settings—in the woods, by the lake, or in a favorite, restful chair by a window.
- The concerns of people and their needs and wants are central to their prayer life as they ask for divine guidance or intervention in the lives of those who need it.

> *So often the impressions I receive from "out there" are accurate, driving my inherent trust in the unseen world. Perhaps other people*

could receive the same messages I do, both from the natural world and from the events of life, if they took the time to notice. As I listen to a friend, attempt to express myself through poetry, or walk through a meadow, I consciously open my mind to what God might be saying to me.

More often than not, God has plenty to say! I think that's why I've been able to bring to fruition my dream of helping other women through my art. For the past five years, I've followed my "hunches," which I believe were really God's advice. The results? A workshop for women in poverty, funded by grants, that virtually no one else thought possible.

—Sondra, 37, artist

Worship

Introverted Feeling types frequently object to the many rules of faith and imposed spiritual methods in spiritual communities because these restrictions can result in people being hurt or ostracized. Most of all, they are attracted to worship in places where consideration of others is key. They prefer environments where the unique needs of individuals are recognized and addressed in special ways.

- By modeling cooperation and inclusion, Introverted Feeling types often unconsciously bring people together for worship in a spirit of harmony and joyful teamwork.

During my childhood, my family participated together in our spiritual community. I enjoyed being with my friends each week, but there were so many requirements—things to memorize, duties to perform, places to be, etc. As I grew older, I took a hard look at all of the rules and regulations that our particular tradition placed upon us. What I saw pushed me further and further away.

I don't like the concept that a few people decide who is in and who is out. We were taught that all other faiths, even those very close to our tradition, were wrong and to be avoided. Instead of nurturing all people and helping them grow, the authorities' attitude was, "Just do as we say!" I certainly didn't want to do as they did. Eventually, I left that place to claim for myself what is really important to me as a spiritual person.

—Caleb, 47, independent contractor

- The joy of deep understanding, the communion between self and others, and the personal relationship to the Creator are often facets of Introverted Feeling worship.
- Attending large-group learning or worship experiences can be positive experiences *if* Introverted Feeling types don't have to share personal information or talk with others too soon about their spirituality. Introverted Feeling types prefer being lost in a crowd.

Though I am very happy in my spiritual community, I find the "coffee time" awkward and uncomfortable. I feel very self-conscious even though I can sometimes get into a great conversation. More often than not, it is an unsatisfactory experience for me—milling around, wondering how to connect.
—Bjorn, 43, human resources

Study

Introverted Feeling types usually learn best by observation, reflection, or insight. When they want to learn about spiritual matters, they tend to reflect deeply on the issue at hand, looking for the impact on people or on the values involved.

- Introverted Feeling types often seek a deep understanding of the values and beliefs of others.

I think I was born with a hunger to feed my spiritual self as well as my physical self. I used to read books about Gandhi, St. Joan of Arc, and different religious movements around the world, fascinated by how ordinary people could garner the courage to take such stands. I often checked out biblical encyclopedias, the Koran and its explanations, as well as other sacred texts—all done privately because I felt the need to know for myself about different leaders and spiritual belief systems.

People are sometimes amazed to hear that I started what became my life's work when still a teenager. I learned early on what I value—helping others find soulwork that is personally meaningful and that honors their search, whatever the source. It's a goal worth pursuing for a lifetime.
—Michael, 55, Unitarian minister

- Introverted Feeling types might study topics that provide insights or ideas that bring faith to life. Study choices include workshops with a spiritual bent on marriage, finances, or parenting. Some Introverted Feeling types ponder the lives of spiritual leaders or personal faith biographies. Others are drawn to mysticism—contemplating the unseen.

  Our men's group once did a seminar on time management. The materials were full of suggestions that could be implemented immediately. The presenters made us feel as if everyone, not just me, had these problems.
  —Kirby, 32, police officer

- Introverted Feeling types often like to join small, close-knit groups with a few carefully chosen others for conversation focused on applying spirituality to their lives.

  My wife and I belonged to a small study group for seven years. There were just four couples, and during those years we supported each other through major, traumatic events. It was a highly significant part of our connection to our spiritual community and was also extremely helpful in our lives.
  —Dan, 59, physical therapist

Service

Tender and vulnerable themselves, Introverted Feeling types typically notice the hurts of others and quietly assist in any way they can. Generally, this concern for people, especially the less fortunate, is at the root of their spirituality.

- Many people have been blessed through the efforts of Introverted Feeling types without knowing it. Many Introverted Feeling types feel closest to God when they can bring a meal, fix a car for someone, offer insight on personal issues, or help another's faith journey. They usually observe just what others need and then provide it, at the right time in the right way, often to the surprise of others. They tend to know instinctively when to act and when to wait, what to say and when to keep quiet.

- Other Introverted Feelers find quiet, ongoing roles in their churches or synagogues, such as tending gardens, running sound systems, or caring for children.
- Service that involves ministering to those whose needs are unmet and offering life-giving, personalized resources appeals to Introverted Feeling types. This help may include involvement in human rights, equal access to education, or other social issues. Their passion is often ignited by the hope that they can bring the world toward greater congruence with their values. Sharing with others in times of need often deepens their respect for the quiet acts of courage and altruism they see.

Other Forms of Soulwork

With their naturally spiritual nature, Introverted Feeling types find the spiritual life rich and full and seldom question its role in their lives. Introverted Feeling types also tend to be naturally compassionate and empathetic.

- People generally feel comfortable confiding in Introverted Feeling types because of their ability to listen, their obvious concern for nurturing the spiritual in others, and their openness to the inexplicable.

  Sometimes I ponder why people will share their spiritual insights, issues, or personal concerns with me, even in settings that have no apparent content or discussion of spirituality. Somehow people sense that I think about such things and they risk trusting me with what seems to be intimate knowledge.
  —Corrinne, 56, research scientist

- Soulwork comes from living their lives consistently with their values, thus enabling them to move out into the world, independent of prevailing opinions, with determination and persistence.
- Creative endeavors can also allow Introverted Feeling types to express their values or spirituality, through artistic, literary, or musical works.

  In my spare time, I quilt. There are so many possible and creative ways to do quilts that I am never bored or boxed in. And as much as I feel the quiet enjoyment and peace that comes by doing the actual work, I also find a great deal of pleasure in giving the finished quilts to family members. It is rewarding to see their joy in knowing they have something entirely unique—my quilt for them.
  —John, 56, quality assurance manager

In short, Introverted Feeling spirituality helps us all remember that

- quiet service can bring us close to God,
- faith and soulwork are part of everyday life,
- living up to our ideals and values is vital in each effort we pursue,
- finding ways to intimately connect with our Creator helps our soulwork come alive in every aspect of life.

The Second Half of Life's Spiritual Journey

While Introverted Feeling is about living life according to deeply held values and having a personal relationship with God, eventually life grows short. Or, as do all personalities, the Introverted Feeling types begin to wonder whether they have found sufficient meaning and purpose. Are they bringing about the changes their values call for?

Often at this stage, Introverted Feeling types have developed their natural spiritual path. Then, richness comes through their inferior function, Extraverted Thinking. This involves

- defining and clarifying truth and universal principles in an impartial manner;
- bringing intellectual and philosophical insights to spiritual questions;
- examining the systems and structures of their beliefs or applying logical reasoning to their decisions and values;
- allowing doubts to be the catalyst in searching for new understanding, asking critical questions, and analyzing different explanations.

While they may continue many of their favorite methods of soulwork, here are some examples of what they found as they journeyed on into Extraverted Thinking:

> It's been a long time since I questioned my spiritual precepts. I tended to voice that all paths have merit, so I wasn't very motivated to look more deeply. Now, though, I enjoy the process of questioning in order to understand more clearly the spiritual path I have chosen.

> I decided that it was time to act on what I believe! I initiated a new outreach group, recruited its members, and even ran all of the organizational meetings. Before, I might have attempted to act

alone; now I want to actively convince others to follow my plan!

My beliefs and values are now a tool as I try to objectively analyze my spiritual convictions and make choices about my activities. I defined several logical criteria to clarify the best use of my time and narrowed down my charity work to the two most deserving projects.

I finally took a rigorous class on the main teachings of my religion. The lecturer presented logical arguments to prove our major tenets. I now feel more able to explain my beliefs to others. Her logic gave a structure to the things that I've thought about for years.

I used to object to any suggestion that one rule or belief be applied to everyone. Recently, though, I've begun to study some of the laws or precepts that seem to exist in every culture. I want to understand how these maxims came into existence and whether there are other "universal truths" that we should pay attention to.

Any of the Thinking pathways (chapters 7 and 8) can bring this kind of rest and richness to Introverted Feeling types, if they allow their dominant function a time of rest and let the Spirit guide their thoughts and actions.

ISFP

Introversion Sensing
Feeling Perceiving

*Spirituality in the inner world of
personal meaning and application*

Truly I tell you, just as you did it to one of the least of these who are members of my family; you did it to me.
—*Matthew 25:40*

Greatest Gifts

Quietly enjoying life; Balancing their outward tasks with their inward needs in an easygoing, flexible, amiable way; Doing and saying the right thing at the right moment

Role in Community

Putting others at ease while providing altruistic acts of charity on an individual basis to those in need; Offering resourceful, behind-the-scenes assistance for endeavors they support

---

ISFPs tend to be gentle, compassionate, and considerate. They are often modest and self-effacing in their service to others. They seek cooperative, harmonious, and warm home and work environments. They care about all living things. They aid by providing comfortable atmospheres with color, music, flowers, and other personal touches to please others.

Using their dominant function, Introverted Feeling, is the natural starting place for soulwork. However, their auxiliary or second function,

Extraverted Sensing, fosters a need to gather with others, whether in a small group or a large organization.

Soulwork through the Second Function

While ISFPs tend to begin their soulwork in solitude, Extraverted Sensing calls them to experience the sacred in what is immediate and real, while engaging in the active life given to us. ISFPs are drawn to warm and supportive people who can provide concrete examples of the ways in which soulwork has helped them—what those people did and what outcomes resulted.

> *When I go antiquing, I am drawn to the beauty of certain items, but I also think about the history of each piece—where the first owners might have lived, how it might have graced their home, and what their lives might have been like. My grandma's china set began my interest in antiques. Grandma was very spiritual; when I set the table with the same dishes she used, I gain a sense of support. I share her beliefs in God. From her stories I know she gained strength from her spirituality. That same strength is available to me as well.*
> —Kathleen, 31, small-business owner

Some ISFPs find their Extraverted Sensing gives them more awareness of the needs of others.

> *I have a lot in common with the earthworm—and people who don't consider that a noble comparison forget the role that worms play in aerating soil and making it possible for plants to grow strong and healthy. They aren't visible but they do a lot of good. I don't draw attention to myself as I work alongside others, so they are often surprised by the knowledge I have about them and the unique help I can offer when I suddenly pop into the picture.*
> —Jan, 58, nurse

Within these settings, ISFPs might seek to use Extraverted Sensing by engaging in any of the exercises listed for Extraverted Sensing (pages 51-52), with goals such as:

- appreciating the world around them with an awareness of all the beauty in God's creation,
- applying spiritual teachings to daily, practical purposes,
- revisiting the facts of a situation to draw on their common sense,
- enjoying the straightforward gift of just being alive.

What Might Push ISFPs Away from Their Spiritual Path

For ISFPs, soulwork takes place in the midst of an unpretentious yet full life. Several factors can lead ISFPs to believe that their spiritual walk is not as important as those who may be more open or vocal about their soulwork. Common themes we heard from the ISFPs we interviewed included

- having to do too much socializing, sharing in public settings or in open forums. Many ISFPs dislike being put on the spot to express their spiritual beliefs.
- finding it difficult to overcome rejection. When ISFPs have been hurt or cast aside by the criticism or actions of others, they may not wish to be included again.

> *I've been disappointed by many people in my life, so I've avoided those situations that can lead to similar rejection. However, in all of this, there is one constant—I have discovered that God doesn't let me down.*
> —Michelle, 28, dental assistant

- undervaluing themselves or the contributions they make in the spiritual domain. Because ISFPs like to serve behind-the-scenes, they and others may overlook their abilities or contributions.
- struggling to convey the ideals and values they hold so deeply. Others often miss out on the spiritual depths of ISFPs because, at times, it can be difficult for them to articulate something of such great importance.

Trusted spiritual advisors, friends, and family can help ISFPs find an enriching spiritual path by

- selecting or being role models for the kind of spiritual life ISFPs seek;
- allowing them to be in nature, meditating on the spirituality of natural things and experiencing true leisure with time alone for reflection;
- trying different worship styles;
- joining with them in a small group to add structure to their spiritual journey.

When Life Is Difficult

The fourth, or *inferior,* function for ISFPs is Extraverted Thinking. With their emphasis on their deeply rooted values and beliefs, ISFPs can struggle to tap into the Extraverted Thinking realm of objectivity and taking charge.

In times of stress, the inferior function can erupt, changing the ISFP's behavior into a caricature of ESTJs and ENTJs for whom Extraverted Thinking is the *dominant* function. For ISFPs in times of stress, the following circumstances might trigger the inferior function:

- When there are conflicts among those close to them. ISFPs may work feverishly to smooth over conflicts and may withdraw if they perceive that there is too much disharmony or if they feel they could be at fault.

    The rest of my work team calls on me whenever there are disputes. I try to help people see one side or the other and bring down the emotional levels. However, I'd much rather flee when they fight with each other.
    —Alli, 29, preschool teacher

- When a crisis makes their normally private lives more public. ISFPs may become prematurely resigned to a situation if they believe they have lost face.
- When they are pressured to make major decisions with long-range implications. For ISFPs, the process of living is much more important than setting goals. In the midst of a crisis, ISFPs may refuse to look at the big picture, taking each day one step at a time.
- When they sense the possibility of loss or failure in a relationship.

Often, the worst times for ISFPs are when they go beyond their own emotional or physical limits to be of service to others. Their natural tendency to help can become their undoing because in the process they may deny their own needs in the interest of helping others. Perhaps they overused their dominant Feeling function by trying to make everyone happy. Then ISFPs may lose their natural gentle and caring demeanor and become more like an overbearing boss; their inferior function, Extraverted Thinking takes a dark cast.

> *The foundation where I worked was in turmoil. Two department heads had quit just a few days before the main fundraising event of the year. I pitched in, making arrangements, checking on the guest list, finalizing the floral centerpieces—in short, doing the work of three people. Late one evening as I was helping to set up the banquet tables, I started listening to myself lord over the volunteers, berating*

them for crooked fork placements and bringing the wrong name tags.
'This isn't me,' I thought. I was so embarrassed that I simply left. If
I hadn't, I'm sure I would have continued on and chased away any
remaining volunteers!
  —Lisa, 33, recreation manager

In these situations, ISFPs might become uncharacteristically hasty in their actions. They may make critical comments or display abnormally directive or abrupt behavior. Some ISFPs become overly logical or analytical about a situation, perhaps using a faulty reasoning process. When these symptoms appear, a totally different approach to soulwork often helps. ISFPs might *purposefully* pursue Extraverted Thinking. Its *conscious use* requires ISFPs to shut down what is usually easiest—Introverted Feeling—which may have gotten out or control. By doing so, ISFPs can pull back from service to others and work through situations logically with others who can offer support and affirmation.

Ways to consciously engage the Extraverted Thinking function include

- stepping back from the situation, determining through cause-and-effect statements what happened and what universal truths were violated. Some ISFPs memorize certain passages from sacred or secular readings, giving them a basis for remembering what holds true in any situation. Using this approach often stops the cycle of ISFPs' making excuses for the other people involved or feeling depressed or guilty about the situation.

- organizing or reorganizing something that is important or will save time—a computer database, a color-coded system for storage, or perhaps a better format for some business forms. Using efficiency and sound reasoning at these times can help in sorting out other issues while bringing some momentary order as well.

- engaging the mind in activities that require logic. Some ISFPs read mysteries where the clues add up to the right answer, play games such as chess or duplicate bridge that require analysis and strategy, or work double acrostics to remove themselves mentally from the problems at hand.

In the chosen activity, the key is backing away from subjectivity to engage in a process that takes a more logical and objective approach to the situation. As one ISFP put it, "I now understand the personal costs of agreeing too often to serve the needs of others. With this grounding, I feel a new freedom to say *no* to many requests in order to say *yes* to myself and my spiritual life."

As an ISFP, I am thankful for
>my cooperative and considerate nature,
>my enjoyment of life's precious moments,
>my capacity to minister to the hurts I see,
>the ways in which I bring harmony to human endeavors.

When life is difficult, I can find support by
>accomplishing something that enhances my faith in myself;
>being in the world of nature to experience God at work in this world;
>assessing what really happened in tough situations in an objective way, thereby giving myself a fresh start.

To honor myself and my pathway to God, I can
>allow myself time to be spiritual in my own way,
>clarify my values so that I can know best how to serve others,
>define and accept a logical basis for what I take on faith in order to communicate it more easily to others.

INFP

Introversion Intuition Feeling Perceiving

Spirituality in the inner world of the heart and imagination

Do not conform any longer to the pattern of this world, but be transformed by the renewing of your mind.
—Romans 12:2

Greatest Gifts

Being quiet and insightful as they develop their compelling values; Concentrating on issues that matter to people; Shifting the focus from what is to what could be better

Role in Community

Working with others to identify ideals and the worthiness of striving to meet them; Discerning what has meaning for individuals and communities, then leading through the strength of conviction

---

INFPs tend to be inquisitive, gentle, creative, and concerned about the human condition or the common good. They seek to follow their ideals, remind others of what is important in life, and use humor and insight to make their points. INFPs strive to make their inner vision of perfection real in their lives and in the lives of others.

Using their dominant function, Introverted Feeling, is the natural starting place for soulwork. However, their auxiliary or second function, *Extraverted Intuition*, calls them to look to the outer world.

Soulwork through the Second Function

While INFPs tend to begin their spiritual journey in solitude, their auxiliary function of Extraverted Intuition often fosters a need for some sort of community setting, whether a small group or a large organization. Through worship, study, and fellowship, they open themselves to future possibilities and connections with others. In community, they might actively pursue ways to make things better for people and organizations.

INFPs tend to hold their spiritual community accountable to its values, remind others of what is best for the general welfare, and provide behind-the-scenes care. Talking through situations with others often helps INFPs loosen the grip of an entrenched position on a value or issue. This helps them become more open and receptive to change.

Some INFPs use their Extraverted Intuition to gain new insights.

> *I had decided that one of several overseas opportunities was the best next step for me, but didn't know how to narrow the field. As I walked the beach in search of an answer, I noticed a dog struggling in the surf. I suddenly knew what to do. A long stint in a foreign country would go against my value for a strong family life. I felt I could be overwhelmed, just as the dog was floundering in the ocean. This led me to choose the overseas option with the shortest possible time away from home.*
> —Yasir, 27, architect

Within these settings, INFPs might seek to use Extraverted Intuition by engaging in any of the exercises listed for Intuition (pages 94-98), with goals such as

- exploring future possibilities that allow their ideals to bloom and have an impact on the outer world;
- finding new avenues and untried practices for spiritual expression;
- encouraging and guiding people and organizations by articulating values;
- influencing others by being examples of integrity, loyalty, and support;
- pondering larger ramifications to loosen the grip of an entrenched value or issue.

All of these might help them bring clarity to their beliefs and breadth to their soulwork.

I carry on my spirituality quietly by helping others to discover or understand who they are so they can grow. For these reasons, I've been a volunteer at a homeless shelter, doing what I can to redress injustice even if it's just one person at a time. It truly is a rewarding spiritual experience for me and I hope a helpful experience for them as well.
    —Olivia, 27, musician

What Might Push INFPs Away from Their Spiritual Path

With their desire for a deeply rooted system of beliefs, several factors can lead INFPs to believe that their spiritual walk is too idealistic for the real world. Common themes we heard from the INFPs we interviewed included

- being with people who are dogmatic, rigid, or judgmental in their spirituality.
- being misunderstood or having their spiritual experiences discounted. INFPs may have difficulty finding other people who can relate to their understanding of the mystical aspects of life. Others may accuse them of not being grounded, or worse.

I believe that God often speaks to me, using simple things in nature and small events in my life. I seldom share these insights with other people, though, for I am usually misunderstood.
    —Ira, 48, chef

- Finding out that someone or something has crossed their spiritual values by discrediting or betraying their spiritual community or belief system.

I have spent much of my life out in the world, speaking and acting for my beliefs in ways that go decidedly against my way of being. I must be consistent with my internal values to the point of being independent of prevailing opinions. At my best, I do this as gently as possible without criticizing or demeaning others. I'm determined and persistent, yet quiet unless that approach fails to create the changes I clearly see need to be made.
    —Kirsten, 67, retired counselor

- endeavoring to bring the perfection they believe is possible to their spiritual journey. INFPs sometimes get so caught up in their aspirations and desire for wholeness that they willingly search for better spiritual beliefs, ideas, or disciplines, never really settling on any one practice or faith.

Trusted spiritual advisors, friends, and family and can help INFPs find an enriching spiritual path by

- describing their own deeply held beliefs in an authentic fashion as material for INFPs' reflection;
- understanding the private quality of spirituality for INFPs and providing the needed empathy and openness;
- living by one's values, not out of necessity but with true conviction;
- offering new challenges for external expressions of vision and ideals.

When Life Is Difficult

The fourth, or *inferior*, function for INFPs is Extraverted Thinking. With their inner focus on what matters most and their way of finding a larger meaning or purpose, INFPs can struggle to use Extraverted Thinking for objectivity and truth.

In times of stress, the inferior function can erupt, changing the INFP's behavior into a caricature of ESTJs and ENTJs for whom Extraverted Thinking is the *dominant* function. For INFPs in times of stress, the following circumstances might trigger the inferior function of Thinking:

- When the atmosphere or relationship deteriorates into attack, backbiting, or hypocrisy. INFPs may choose to withdraw if the situation is so far out of hand that they believe there is no opportunity for change.
- When INFPs accommodate the wishes of others in order to retain the relationship or to ensure harmony. Their desire for acceptance may encourage them to hang on to a relationship, leading them to be at war with themselves for doing so—not accepting the reality of the situation.
- When people seem indifferent to the problems of others, leave them isolated or treat them poorly.

It's quite painful to me when people seem callous or indifferent to the needs and hurts of others, especially when they might be to blame. I know that life is too short to try to change everything, so I've learned the hard way to choose my battles and seek others who treat people well and care about them as much as I do.

—Althea, 28, medical student

- When their values compel them to lead or speak up, yet the desired outcome is not achieved. Generally INFPs prefer not to take a direct, out-in-front leadership role. However, when their values or people close to them are threatened, beware—a strong leader will emerge!

Often the worst times for INFPs are when they become too intent on their own point of view or conclusions. Perhaps they overused their dominant function, Introverted Feeling, getting entrenched in their own beliefs, becoming unwilling to admit other viewpoints, and moving toward isolation from others. Their inferior function, Extraverted Thinking, takes a dark cast.

> *I wanted to serve on the ethics committee of my professional organization because its integrity was so very important to me. Soon I became the spokesperson for the group and traveled and wrote extensively about ethical behaviors and situations. I realized when people started referring to me as the leader of the "ethical Gestapo," that I had become too one-sided and harsh—something I so dislike in others!*
> —Nancy, 59, counselor

In these situations, INFPs might be overly objective or closed off to new viewpoints and information. They may verbalize critical and negative remarks about others (and sometimes about themselves) or situations. When these symptoms appear, a totally different approach to soulwork often helps. INFPs might *purposefully* pursue Extraverted Thinking. Its *conscious use* requires that INFPs shut down what is usually easiest—Introverted Feeling—which may have gotten out of control. By doing so, INFPs can look to the external world to determine the most logical outcome to a given situation.

Ways to consciously engage the Extraverted Thinking function include

- seeking the advice of a trusted friend or colleague to work through the pros and cons of different courses of action, discuss rational explanations for the behavior of others, and objectively look for the cause-and-effect of the crisis. With that assistance, INFPs can often develop a logical plan of attack—and then can give it one more test by asking, "What does my heart say?"
- using a ranking system to choose between various alternatives. By listing all the needs or criteria and assigning number values to the options, the correct course of action often becomes clear.

- engaging the mind in activities that require logic. Some INFPs read mysteries, play games such as chess or duplicate bridge that require analysis and strategy, or work double acrostics to remove themselves mentally from the problems at hand.

In the chosen activity, the key is backing away from overanalyzing and criticizing and, instead, engaging in a process that allows them to appreciate all the good there is in people and the world. As one INFP put it, "The dispassionate language of logic used to strike me as unspiritual. Now, however, I find that it allows me to articulate my deeply held beliefs much more clearly and in ways that make it easier for others to understand."

As an INFP, I am thankful for
> my idealism and hope for the world;
> my intense ideas, which provide me energy to live life deeply and abundantly;
> my ever-present awareness of the beauty, liminality, and synchronicity of life's experiences;
> the way I value the importance of the spiritual journey and the things that give meaning to life.

When life is difficult, I can find support by
> asking, "What is most important to me?" and then making a change—sometimes even a radical change,
> using a trusted person to help me see things objectively,
> dialoguing with myself through journaling or art or by meditating while walking in nature.

To honor myself and my pathway to God, I can
> create solitude to tap into my awareness of the spiritual part of my life,
> live with personal authenticity and integrity,
> add logic and objectivity in order to more clearly understand my heartfelt soulwork.

CONCLUSION

BEING WHOLLY SPIRITUAL

S ixteen types, four major paths to spirituality. Does this mean that we each need to chart a distinct spiritual path? Throw out traditions and start anew? Form separate spiritual communities? Have spiritual leaders adapt to each of these paths? Our conclusion is a certain NO.

In spirituality, traveling down just one path can be the route to stagnation, offering little chance of surprise, challenge, or development. For all types, spiritual wholeness develops when we see "how the other half lives"—when we allow for insights and information from spiritual experiences that are different from our initial, more natural paths.

However, for people whose natural paths depart from traditional forms of spirituality—such as those *Sensing* types who prefer finding God spontaneously in the midst of their enjoyment of all that God has given us; those *Intuitive* types who break with tradition in favor of innovation and new experiences; those *Thinking* types who are chastened for their customary skepticism; and those *Feeling* types who rail against systems that seem to shut out those who are in most need of help—for everyone's sake, we need to rethink what it means to be spiritual. Otherwise we may lose the opportunity to find avenues that lead toward wholeness and spiritual fulfillment. As you finish these pages, take a moment to consider how to best nurture your own soul as well as the spirit in each of us.

Inviting Everyone to Wholeness

What shoulds and oughts do you or those around you bring to the realm of soulwork? Consider the practices and traditions of your personal spirituality or those of your spiritual community within the framework of Sensing, Intuitive, Thinking, and Feeling soulwork. Sometimes the changes that will allow each type to feel at home are simple, as we heard from the many people we talked to in the course of writing *SoulTypes*.

- One of our friends detests her church's tradition of standing during the worship service to greet or share the Peace with strangers. "If only the minister would say, 'Share *with a friend or* a stranger,' I'd feel comfortable."

- Another person we interviewed expressed the need not to be judged for "skipping school" once in awhile. "I like my study group, but sometimes on a winter day my soul would be better fed by setting our lessons aside for a nature hike."

- "I want the freedom to *not* take a stand," several commented. "Issues aren't always clear; circumstances change. Please allow some of my beliefs to be cloudy."

- "If I try to talk about spirituality, my thoughts get muddled. I have to keep it to myself because it is so personal" was another common plea.

For every tradition, practice, or form of spirituality, stay open-minded and allow people to react in their own ways to the routines and customs that others view as perfectly normal.

Your Personal Path to Spiritual Richness

However, before you work to increase understanding in those around you, take one more look at your own soulwork. Are you at peace with the requirements you place on yourself? Have you discovered and defined the essentials of your type of spirituality? Are there ways in which your spiritual life could be augmented or deepened?

As an ENFP (Sandra) and INFJ (Jane), our most natural paths to soulwork are through our Intuition and Feeling functions. For us, the essence of spirituality is adding insight and understanding to our faith, then sharing it with others. If the two of us fail to nurture these deep spiritual values, our soulwork can quickly go dry. However, our soulwork would be incomplete if we stopped here.

We both need to add *Thinking* to our spirituality. A sprinkling of skepticism and discernment is vital to our teaching, our writing, and our ability to successfully apply our spirituality to what we do and to our decisions.

And finally we both need our inferior function, *Sensing* to pull ourselves away from our imaginations and innovations and back to the practical applications of faith, the everyday delights of what God has created, the value of consistency in some pursuits, and the richness and history of spiritual traditions.

Take some time to articulate for yourself the vital practices of your soulwork. Reread the natural paths of your personality type to find those core purposes or approaches that draw you to spirituality. But then look at the paths of a type very different from you—your exact opposite (for example, ENFPs would read the ISTJ chapter.) What could you gain? What might you be missing?

Often, the key to understanding isn't adapting to everyone else—it is understanding the genuine psychological differences, comprehending the spiritual viewpoint of another, gaining knowledge from a changed perspective, or discovering new forms of soulwork that turn out to be avenues to meaning and growth for you.

May these pages help you

rejoice in the special spiritual journey that will best engage your soul;

grant new freedom for others to take a different path;

create the patterns of soulwork that add faith, truth, meaning, and support to every step of life's journey.

SUGGESTIONS FOR A FIVE-SESSION GROUP STUDY

T he following activities and questions are intended for group use, although individuals can easily adapt them for personal study. They are written for all group participants, but to facilitate the process and discussion invite someone to serve as leader.

Session 1: Identifying Your Own Spiritual Path

Allow each person to discern his or her psychological type. You may use the introductory chapters of *SoulTypes* or, with the help of a qualified practitioner, take the MBTI®.

Questions for Discussion or Self-Reflection

1. Looking back, what are some of the high points in your spiritual journey (think outside as well as within the box of organized religion)?
2. Have you felt judged at certain times? Made to feel that you weren't spiritual? What happened?
3. Which definition of spirituality best suits you?
   - Aligning our souls with heart, mind, and body to fulfill one's purpose, believing that reality includes more than the tangible,

and pursuing a relationship with One greater than ourselves (authors' definition)

- Sensitivity or attachment to religious values (*Webster's Dictionary*)
- A devotion to metaphysical matters as opposed to worldly things
- Spirituality may be defined as an individual's sense of peace, purpose, and connection to others and beliefs about the meaning of life (National Cancer Institute)
- Your own:

4. Finish the prompt, "If I could deepen my spiritual walk, then I could . . ."

The Gifts of Each Type
Gather in type-alike groups (those who share the same four letters) and study the first page from the chapter for your type. Then, report to the larger group what you would like them to know about the gifts of your type. If some types have only one person, ask them to be a "group" of one.

Preparation for the Next Meeting
Read the entire chapter for your spiritual path. Discuss your type preferences with someone who knows you well. Make note of the ways in which your own personal soulwork matches the chapter description. What rang most true? Make note of a step toward a deeper spirituality you hope to take as a result of this study.

Session 2: The Eight Type Paths to Soulwork
If the group is small, each person may want to share one thing that stood out from reading about his or her type and spirituality. People also can voice questions that arose for them and mention which others in the group might be able to answer or provide some insights.

Questions for Discussion
1. Which prayer, worship, or study suggestions seemed most rewarding to you? If you have used it, describe your experience.

2. Did the chapter remind you of affirming spiritual experiences? Negative ones? Share these with the group.

3. Did you try any of the spiritual practices? How did they work?

Exploring Each Type

Have each of the four groups (by dominant function) plan an ideal but fictitious retreat or event for soulwork. Each group can decide on location, preferred activities, size of the group, and so forth. Have each group present their ideas to the entire group. Note the differences and similarities.

Preparation for the Next Meeting

Read the summary pages on Sensing and Intuitive spirituality (pages 49-52 and 94-98). Then read the chapter for the type that is your opposite. For example, INFJs read the ESTP chapter to gain an awareness of the different approaches to spirituality.

Session 3: Sensing and Intuitive Soulwork

Group Exercise

Have everyone complete the exercise for Sensing and Intuitive spirituality (page 46). Then, have people form groups:

Those for whom Sensing is the *first function* (ISTJ, ISFJ, ESTP, ESFP)

Those for whom Sensing is the *second function* (ISFP, ISTP, ESFJ, ESTJ)

Those for whom Sensing is the *third function* (INTP, INFP, ENTJ, ENFJ)

Those for whom Sensing is the *fourth function* (INFJ, INTJ, ENFP, ENTP)

Ask the groups to consider:

1. Was the exercise easy or difficult, and why?

2. What about the exercise helped them tap into their type of spirituality?

3. What insights did they gain?

Have each group describe their insights to the entire group.

Exploring Your Type

Choose three exercises under "Suggestions for Sensing Spirituality" (page 50) and "Suggestions for Intuitive Spirituality" (page 95) for group discussion.

Instruct each person whose dominant or auxiliary function is Sensing to choose one from among the three Sensing exercises and those whose dominant or auxiliary function is Intuition to choose one from among the three Intuitive exercises, then try it.

Allow at least twenty minutes for each person to work through his or her chosen exercise. If space allows, spread out—even go outdoors.

As people come back together, join with others who chose the same exercise for small group discussion. Some questions for the groups to consider are:

1. Was the exercise easy or difficult, and why?
2. What about the exercise helped you tap into your type of spirituality?
3. What insights did you gain?

Each group can then describe each of the experiences and insights to the entire group.

Sensing and Intuitive Soulwork

Review as a group the summary pages for Sensing and Intuitive soulwork (pages 49-52 and 94-98). Discuss:

1. What surprises are there about what each group considers spiritual?
2. How might Sensing types and Intuitive types struggle or flourish within this group study experience? Within this spiritual setting or community?

Preparation for the Next Meeting

Sensing types can try one of the eighteen soulwork suggestions for Intuitive types and vice versa.

Session 4: Thinking and Feeling Spirituality

Discuss your experiences with trying the opposite soulwork suggestions. For example, Sensing types share what it was like to try an exercise oriented toward Intuitive types and vice versa.

Group Exercise

To complete the exercise for Thinking and Feeling Spirituality (page 142) have people form groups:

Those for whom Thinking is the *first function* (ISTP, INTP, ESTJ, ENTJ)

Those for whom Thinking is the *second function* (ISTJ, INTJ, ESTP, ENTP)

Those for whom Thinking is the *third function* (INFJ, ISFJ, ESFP, ENFP)

Those for whom Thinking is the *fourth function* (ISFP, INFP, ESFJ, ENFJ)

Give the groups twenty minutes to discuss the question, "What should Wiesenthal have done and why?" Ask them to record the *process* of their discussion—what thoughts and concerns were raised and in what order, not just their final answer. Then compare the groups' responses.

Alternate Exercise

Choose three of the "Suggestions for Thinking Spirituality" and three of the "Suggestions for Feeling Spirituality" for group discussion

Instruct each person whose dominant or auxiliary function is Thinking to choose one of the above suggested Thinking exercises and those whose dominant or auxiliary function is Feeling to choose one from among the suggested Feeling exercises above and then try it.

Allow at least twenty minutes for each person to work through his or her chosen exercise. If space allows, spread out—even go outdoors.

As people come back together, ask those who chose the same exercise to join together for small group discussion. Some questions to consider are:

1. Was the exercise easy or difficult, and why?
2. What about the exercise helped you tap into your type of spirituality?
3. What insights did you gain?

Each breakout group can then describe each of the experiences and insights to the entire group.

Preparation for the Next Meeting

Read the conclusion of *SoulTypes* (pages 241-43). Come up with a phrase that expresses the essence of your spirituality. (Our example is on page 242-43: "For us, the essence of spirituality is adding insight and understanding to our faith, then sharing it with others.") For enrichment, Thinking types can try one of the eighteen suggestions for Feeling soulwork and vice versa.

Session 5: The Spiritual Journey

Using the chart on page 37, consider the type dynamics (order of preferences) of the group. How many dominant Sensing, Intuitive, Thinking, and Feeling types are there? Break into discussion groups by dominant functions (the first preference listed in the chart for each type). If the group is large (more than thirty people), divide further by grouping the Introverted Sensing types, Extraverted Sensing types, Introverted Intuitive types, and so forth.

Questions for Discussion

Using the summary pages on each of the functions (Sensing, pages 49-52, Intuition, pages 94-98, Thinking, pages 145-49, Feeling, pages 193-98) as a guide, discuss the following:

1. What is your definition of spirituality? What does soulwork look like for your group? When do you feel most spiritual?
2. With what spiritual practices do you struggle the most? What insights into the sources of these struggles did you gain from *Soul-Types*? What, if any, are the relationships to type?

Find the section, "The Second Half of Life's Spiritual Journey" for your spiritual path. Read through the information and the examples of ways people have found rich, new spiritual practices through their fourth function. In small groups, based on your fourth functions (Sensing, Intuition, Thinking, or Feeling), share ideas and examples of using your fourth function to discover new pathways.

For additional insights, consider major spiritual events in your life. How do these events fit with the path of spiritual growth? You might fill in a chart similar to the one below.

My *dominant* function is: Spiritual milestones that reflect my dominant function:

My *auxiliary* function is: Spiritual milestones that reflect my auxiliary function:

My *third* function is: Ways in which I used my third function
                                            in soulwork:

My *inferior* function is: Ways in which my inferior function could
                                            enrich or hinder my soulwork:

    Individually, revisit the phrase describing your spirituality (see Session 4, "Preparation for the Next Meeting"). Commit to one spiritual practice to *continue* fervently and to one spiritual practice to *start* for exploration and experimentation with your soulwork.

    Share each person's commitment to his or her spiritual practices and the phrases that capture the essence of his or her spirituality.

    Do any evaluation or next-step activity that seems appropriate.

APPENDIX B

SUGGESTIONS FOR FURTHER READING

Baab, Lynne M. *Personality Type in Congregations: How to Work with Others More Effectively*. Bethesda, Md.: The Alban Institute, 1998.

Baab, Lynne M. *Embracing Midlife: Congregations as Support Systems*. Bethesda, Md.: The Alban Institute, 1999.

Corlett, Eleanor S., and Nancy B. Millner. *Navigating Midlife: Using Typology as a Guide*. Palo Alto, Calif.: Davies-Black, 1993.

Duncan, Bruce. *Pray Your Way: Your Personality and God*. London: Darton, Longman & Todd, 1993.

Goldsmith, Malcolm. *Knowing Me, Knowing God: Exploring Your Spirituality with Myers-Briggs*. Nashville: Abingdon, 1997.

Hirsh, Sandra Krebs, and Jane A. G. Kise. *Looking at Type and Spirituality*. Gainesville, Fla.: Center for Applications of Psychological Type, 1997.

Kise, Jane A. G., and David Stark. *Working with Purpose: Finding a Corporate Calling for You and Your Business*. Minneapolis: Augsburg Books, 2004.

Kise, Jane A. G., David Stark, and Sandra Krebs Hirsh. *LifeKeys: Discover Who You Are*. 2nd ed. Minneapolis: Bethany House, 2005.

Michael, Chester P., and Marie C. Norrisey. *Prayer and Temperament: Different Prayer Forms for Different Personality Types.* Charlottesville, Va.: Open Door, 1991.

Moore, Thomas. *Care of the Soul: A Guide for Cultivating Depth and Sacredness in Everyday Life.* New York: HarperPerennial, 1994.

Moses, Jeffrey. *Oneness: Great Principles Shared by All Religions.* New York: Fawcett Columbine, 1989.

Mulholland, M. Robert Jr. *Invitation to a Journey: A Road Map for Spiritual Formation.* Downers Grove, Ill.: InterVarsity, 1993.

Myers, Isabel Briggs, and Peter B. Myers. *Gifts Differing.* Palo Alto, Calif.: Davies-Black, 1980.

Quenk, Naomi L. *Was That Really Me? How Everyday Stress Brings Out Our Hidden Personality.* Palo Alto, Calif.: Davies-Black, 2002.

Richardson, Peter Tufts. *Four Spiritualities: Expressions of Self, Expressions of Spirit.* Palo Alto, Calif.: Davies-Black, 1996.

NOTES

Preface
1. Jane A. G. Kise, David Stark, and Sandra Krebs Hirsh, *LifeKeys: Discover Who You Are*, 2nd ed. (Minneapolis: Bethany House, 2005).

Introduction: Pathways, Pursuits, and Practices
1. Sharon Begley with Anne Underwood, "Religion and the brain," *Newsweek*, May 7, 2001, 53–4.
2. Jeffrey Kluger, "Is God in our genes?" *Time*, Oct. 25, 2004, 62.
3. Kenneth L. Woodward, "Faith is more than feeling," *Newsweek*, May 7, 2001, 58.
4. Carl Jung, quoted in *The Quotable Spirit: A Treasury of Religious and Spiritual Questions, from Ancient Times to the 20th Century*, ed. Peter Lorie and Manuela Dunn Mascetti (New York: MacMillan, 1966), 208.
5. Jane A. G. Kise, David Stark, and Sandra Krebs Hirsh, *LifeKeys: Discover Who You Are*, 2nd ed. (Minneapolis: Bethany House, 2005).

Part 1: Understanding Psychological Type
Chapter 2: Growing Toward Wholeness and Meaning
1. Carl Jung, *Modern Man in Search of a Soul*, trans. W. S. Dell and C. F. Baynes (New York: Harcourt, Brace, Jonavich, 1933), 108.

Part 2: Sensing and Intuitive Spirituality

The Paths of Sensing Spirituality

1. Robert Browning, *Pippa Passes* (1841), pt. 1, quoted in John Bartlett, *Familiar Quotations,* 16th ed. (Boston: Little, Brown, 1992).

The Paths of Intuitive Spirituality

1. Henry Ward Beecher, *Proverbs from Plymouth Pulpit* (Charles Burnet & Co., 1887).
2. Henry David Thoreau, *Journal,* July 14, 1852.

Part 3: Thinking and Feeling Spirituality

Introduction: The Sunflower Exercise

1. Simon Wiesenthal, *The Sunflower: On the Possibilities and Limits of Forgiveness* (New York: Schocken Press, 1997), 54. After the war, Wiesenthal solicited responses from several religious figures, including the Dali Lama, Matthew Fox, and Rabbi Harold Kushner. What should Wiesenthal have done? *The Sunflower* contains their responses.

The Paths of Thinking Spirituality

1. Buddha, *Dhammapada* in *The Quotable Spirit: A Treasury of Religious and Spiritual Questions, from Ancient Times to the 20th Century,* ed. Peter Lorie and Manuela Dunn Mascetti (New York: MacMillan, 1966), 257.
2. Kahlil Gibran, *Sand and Foam* (New York: Alfred A. Knopf, 1926), quoted in John Bartlett, *Familiar Quotations,* 651.
3. Simone Weil, quoted in *The Quotable Spirit,* 240.
4. George Fox, quoted in *Devotional Classics,* edited by Richard Foster and James Bryan Smith (San Francisco: HarperSanFrancisco, 1993), 220.
5. George Appleton, ed., *The Oxford Book of Prayer,* (Oxford: Oxford University Press, 1985), 115.

Chapter 7: Extraverted Thinking: The Analytical Spiritual Path

1. Bruce Duncan, *Pray Your Way: Your Personality and God* (London: Darton, Longman & Todd, 1993), 115.

The Paths of Feeling Spirituality

1. Ella Wheeler Wilcox, "The World's Need," *The Century,* June 1895, 185.
2. Jeffrey Moses, *Oneness: Great Principles Shared by All Religions* (New York: Fawcett Columbine, 1989), 38.
3. Prayer of St. Francis, quoted in John Bartlett, *Familiar Quotations,* 16th ed. (Boston: Little, Brown, 1992), 123.
4. Pattinatar, as quoted in *The Oxford Book of Prayer* (Oxford: Oxford University Press, 1985), 290.